Walter Moorcroft
Memories of Life and Living

To my wife Liz and all my family

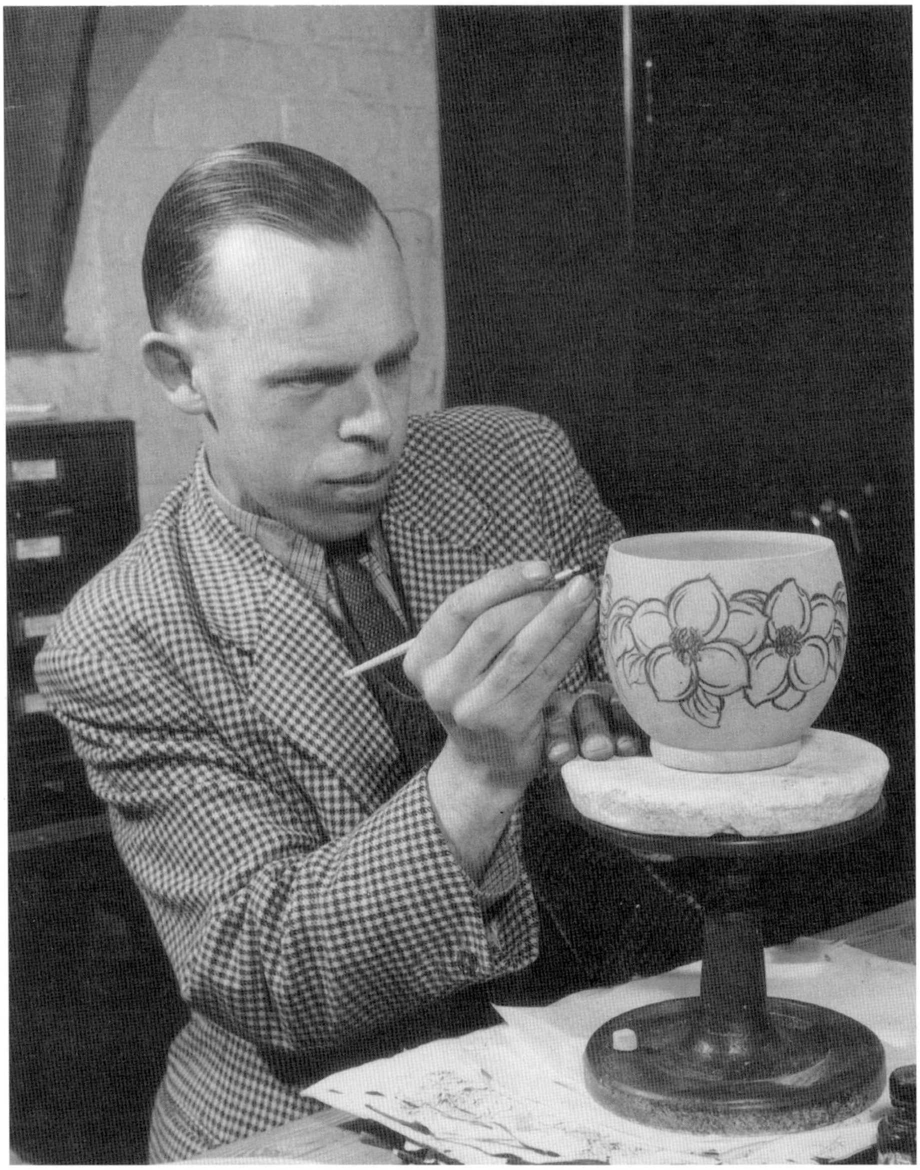

Making the brush drawing for my development of the *Clematis* design, 1953.

Walter Moorcroft
Memories of Life and Living

RICHARD DENNIS
1999

ACKNOWLEDGEMENTS

The idea of writing my autobiography had never occurred to me but my family continually urged me to commit my reminiscences to paper and I began to do so in the autumn of 1996. At around the same time, my wife and I spent the weekend with Richard and Sally Dennis at their home in Somerset. During a conversation with Sally, Liz happened to mention my new 'project'. Richard overheard and said in his usual quiet manner, 'I would like to publish that...' And so it was.

I would like to thank the following people: Malcolm Haslam for his advice and encouragement in the early stages; Ken Bowen of the Message Centre, Hanley, for organising the typing of my original manuscript; Sue Evans, my editor, for her patient appraisal of my efforts; Magnus Dennis for the colour photography; Wendy Wort and the team at Richard Dennis Publications; *The Evening Sentinel*, Stoke-on-Trent; Tony Priestley for loaning his views of Stoke; Cynthia Findlay, Sandy and Libby Hill, Richard and Nan Jaroszonck, John McGie, Joanne McPhee, Dave Simmons and Bill Teskey for lending their pots for photography; and my wife Liz for her unfailing support and good-humoured acceptance of the inevitable upheavals caused by Richard and his entourage who had frequent cause to enjoy the warmth of her hospitality.

Edited by Sue Evans
Colour photography by Magnus Dennis
Production by Wendy Wort
Print, design and reproduction by Flaydemouse, Yeovil, Somerset
Published by Richard Dennis, The Old Chapel, Shepton Beauchamp, Somerset TA19 OLE, England

ISBN 0 903685 71 X

British Library Cataloguing-in-Publication Data. A catalogue record for this book is available from the British Library

Contents

Foreword

The idea for this book by my father-in-law, Walter Moorcroft, dates back to a favourite family walk on 'The Headland' close to Trearddur Bay, Anglesey in May 1995. Liz, Sara and our children were a little ahead while Walter and I were deep in conversation. He was reminiscing about the Second World War, describing being driven through London on top of an open three-ton truck containing motorbikes, prior to setting off on missions into France after D-Day. For many years the family and I had been trying to persuade Walter to write down his fascinating stories. On this occasion, I was determined that one of us would finally succeed in persuading him to 'put pen to paper'.

This story about Walter's life is highly readable. It tells of his excellent leadership of Moorcroft Pottery between 1945 and 1987 and the factory's development, both in design and methods of production, during a period of great technological change. Walter's memories of the twentieth century include many humorous and perceptive insights into social history, in particular his time at Rugby School and life in the thirties, and his experiences in the Second World War.

These memoirs illustrate Walter's many interests. There is the emphasis on creativity and his love of colour as seen in his designs and in his choice of bright shirts and ties. Walter is a great raconteur and his love of language – he is fluent in French, German and Spanish – comes shining through. Today, he experiences a little difficulty with his knee joints which he puts down to having regularly played nine sports during his lifetime. Walter's abiding love of sport is demonstrated by the fact that he continued to play golf competitively until the age of eighty!

This book is a testament to Walter Moorcroft the family man, and his love of those around him. To his family and friends, Walter is both a gentleman and a gentle man. We are sure that you will find these memoirs as fascinating to read as we have found them to listen to.

Paul Morrissey,
January 1999

With Queen Mary at the British Industries Fair, 1947.

Memories of Life and Living

Childhood in Trentham

We caught sticklebacks with jam jars...

I was born in Trentham, a village in Staffordshire, in the early hours of the morning on the 12th February 1917, when the outcome of the First World War was still in the balance.

Trentham Hotel, 1912.

My parents met in 1912 when they were both living at the Trentham Hotel. My father was producing his early Moorcroft designs at the factory of James Macintyre in Burslem and my mother, who was one of the early lady factory inspectors, had been transferred from the cotton mills of Lancashire to the pottery industry in Stoke-on-Trent. Her knowledge of working conditions had a considerable influence on the design of the Moorcroft factory which opened in 1913. They married in April 1913 and bought a house called Glendair in Albert Drive, Trentham, which was to be my home until I married in 1946.

My mother, Florence.

I have no prodigiously early memories except for one of my mother in her double bed in the front bedroom of Glendair. She was sitting up with her hair loose and a slightly pendulous breast with a large brown nipple escaping from her cream nightdress. How young I was at the time I have no idea. I was just content and warm and the scene has remained imprinted on my mind.

During the 1920s there were no road names or street lamps in Trentham. The village shop was Littler's at Hem Heath post office and was run by Mr and Mrs Littler who sold everything from groceries to haberdashery – their son, Dick, also owned a taxi with a shiny bonnet. Further down the lane was Bickerton's, which sold every kind of biscuit displayed in large square tins with glass lids. Mr Birks came each morning in his pony and trap to deliver the milk which was carried in a highly-polished churn from which he ladled the required quantity with a copper baler. Once a week Mr Oram came with his horse and cart loaded with vegetables and a limited choice of seasonal fruit.

Littler's shop in Hem Heath, c1920.

Glendair was illuminated by gaslights which were supplemented here and there by oil lamps with a glass chimney in the centre and had to be lit carefully otherwise they would smoke and turn black. The gas lights had a single mantle protected by a glass globe and extended from the wall on a metal bracket. These were lit by matches or spills, kept in spill vases, which were a regular part of household equipment. A major development was the installation of central light fittings in the dining and drawing rooms. These had three mantles and silk shades with a beaded fringe. The gas was lit by a 'by-pass' (later called a pilot light) when a fragile chain was pulled to turn on the supply.

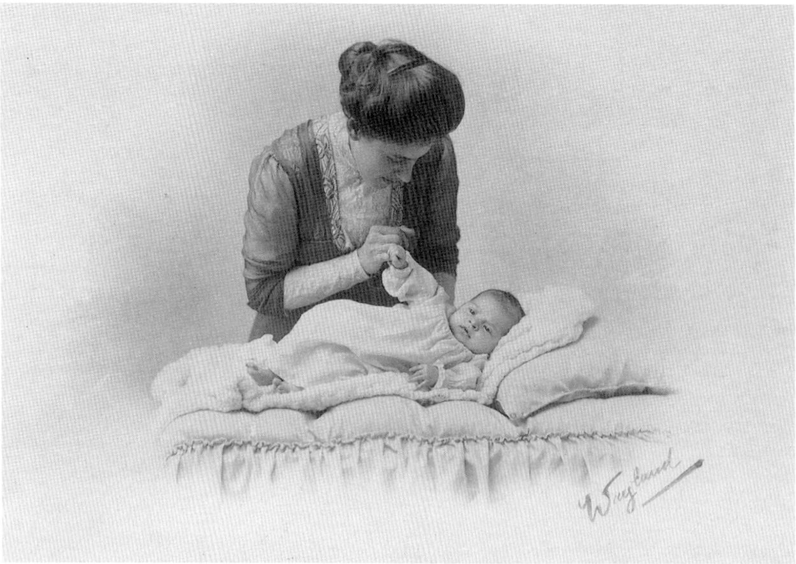

Mother and baby Beatrice, 1915.

In the dining room was a mahogany table and heavy mahogany chairs with large porcelain casters which taught you not to tip back on your chair. If you did so, the chair shot backwards on its casters, its heavy mahogany frame hitting you on the head. From the dining room, French windows opened on to a gravel path leading to a 'Snowball' tree at the bottom of the garden. The painted fence alongside the path was a faded green and Graham Baines, who lived next door, would climb up his side and look over to see if my sister Beatrice and I wanted to play. When Graham's sister was born, I commented on the number of serviettes on their washing-line, thereby causing much adult amusement, the reason for which I failed to appreciate.

Beatrice was two-and-a-half years older than me and, having a vivid imagination, was often the ringleader in our escapades. The garden was our playground and other children were welcome as mother preferred to know where we were although she was not always aware of what we were doing. One day, an anxious call from a neighbour informed her that I was making my way along a very narrow ledge outside an upstairs' window. We had a lean-to cycle shed at the back of the house and spent hours playing on its roof. This proved to be safer than playing inside which was the scene of my first injury when our cat had given birth to kittens. While scrambling up to see them I impaled my leg just above the knee on a rusty nail projecting from a packing case. Once the agony was over it became my proudly-displayed scar and I still have it today.

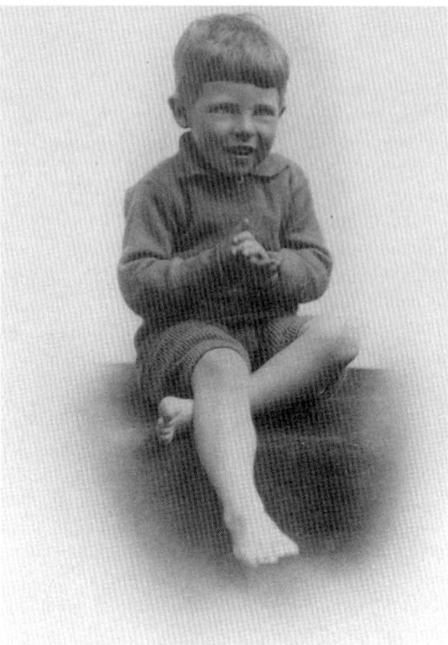

Myself, aged three.

A rope hanging from a branch of the May tree in our front garden provided our first swing. When we grew out of this a pair of sturdy timber-built swings were put up in the back garden and a favourite trick was to leap from the swing at its highest point to see how far I could propel myself across the lawn. Our garden was the scene for all kinds of games and activities (such as putting worms into jars of water to watch them wriggle) but my mother also believed in keeping us on the move. We went for long walks along the canal bank with strict instructions to stand aside when a horse-drawn barge went past, in order to keep clear of the tow rope which might drag us into the water. Water rats swam in the canal and kingfishers provided flashes of colour as they darted to and fro along the bank. We often walked as far as the lock keeper's cottage where we passed the time of day and watched the lock fill and empty as the barges went through carrying their mysterious cargoes either to the Potteries or to destinations further up the Trent and Mersey canal.

We caught sticklebacks with jam jars attached to string and had picnics by the streams which took the overflow from the canal where, with great triumph, we might catch a fish using a net instead of a jam jar. My greatest catch was a crested newt which enjoyed a briefly extended life in our aquarium at home. We actually acquired fishing rods from Dutton's Toy Shop in Stone but, baited with bread, they didn't appeal to the fish – the jam jar was best. Another area for jam jar fishing for tadpoles and water boatmen was the pond in the middle of the 'froggie fields' which lay between Leyfield Road, just around the corner from Albert Drive and the canal. 'Froggie fields' was our private name for a meadow which became a sea of buttercups and kingcups and was alive with frogs in due season.

Barlaston Road, Trentham, c1920.

Parallel with the canal was the Barlaston Road which was the starting point for many of our expeditions. It was unsurfaced and the rare passing of a car was followed by a cloud of dust. The hedges were high on both sides of the road and the verge, in many cases, was wide enough to play hide-and-seek in and out of the bushes. The first point of interest was a bridge where the stream from the canal ran under the road along a brick-lined tunnel and through which it was possible to run, jumping from side to side over the water – most exciting! Next we came to a farm with a large duck pond beside the road, populated with ever hungry ducks, and from there on to a ford where another stream sparkled its way across the road. Two miles further on, the road reached Barlaston and branched left to the station and uphill to the village. We called the straight-on way 'fairyland' as it was a wilderness of trees and mysterious undergrowth with a narrow track which wound its way, seemingly for ever, until you came to Stone.

The Downs, Stone, c1920.

Sometimes we took the train to Barlaston and made the long haul up the hill to the Barlaston Downs known locally as the 'Downs banks'. These formed two partially wooded ridges covered in bracken with a stream running through the valley between, where we paddled and made dams with loose stones from the stream bed. At the approach to the Downs was a massive oak tree which was a favourite haunt as, five or six feet above the ground, it became hollow making a spacious den within its huge trunk. Our expeditions usually finished with a picnic on the Downs or a walk across Barlaston village green to one of the cottages which served afternoon teas. We then began our trek back to the station – fortunately downhill all the way.

Trentham Hall was the home of the Duke of Sutherland throughout the nineteenth century and, as he owned a great deal of land in north Staffordshire, most of the local population were his tenants. Trentham Gardens was opened to the public in about 1911 after the Duke left the district. Italian gardens with close-cut lawns and intricate designs of low box hedges interspersed by huge fountains led down to the mile-long lake which was surrounded by semi-wild woodland. The entrance to the gardens was through the stables down by the church, a mile's walk away and, in the early days, a large pushchair

Trentham Hall.

Entrance to Trentham Gardens.

The Italian Garden with the lake beyond.

was a great help in covering the distance. The lake was the great attraction and we often hired a rowing boat – flat-bottomed for safety – and rowed out to the island where, on landing, we moored the boat carefully so that we were not marooned. I remember one occasion when we rowed to the far end of the lake, moored on the lakeside, and ate a marvellous picnic with the sunlight coming through the trees which were overhanging the water.

Spring Valley, Trentham, c1915.

As a special treat we used to make the long trip, aided by the pushchair, around the far side of the lake to Spring Valley where crystal-clear water which we could drink gushed out between rocks, first into a pool and then down a fast flowing stream into the lake. Once, I excelled myself by falling into the stream and my mother had to cover me with assorted items of dry clothing to get me home. To save carrying picnics we often went to the tearooms in the orangery, a beautifully proportioned building adjoining Trentham Hall. Later this was converted into a ballroom, but in the 1920s had a sandy gravel floor and orange trees still growing in square wooden containers, the once green paint faded to a sort of greyish-blue.

The Tea Rooms, a favourite place for a treat.

Trentham Church and Sculpture Gallery, c1920.

We always had 'Tea' – bread, butter, jam and cakes – and to this day I can hear the welcome sound of china clinking on the tray as the waitress carried it across the rather uneven surface of the sand and gravel. We were often served by Mrs Tansley whose family had been tenants of the Duke of Sutherland for years. She wore a black dress, white apron and a starched white cap. When we were old enough, we were taken to Trentham Church which had been the Duke's place of worship. The church stood within the estate and had a door on the far side which led into the gardens. On a summer's day the door was left open and fountains could be seen sparkling brightly in the Italian garden leading down to the lake, in sharp contrast to the ecclesiastic gloom inside the church. Before the sermon started, mother would quietly lead us into the gardens and across the river to Mr Nicklin's gate. (Mr Nicklin lived in the lodge beside the gate and knew us well as holders of season tickets.) This not only provided an escape from church but reduced the dull walk home by at least a quarter of a mile.

In 1923 there was a hard winter and Trentham lake was frozen – a rare occurrence. Mother bought us Norwegian wooden skates which had very shallow blades to ensure that you did not easily turn your ankle. I don't remember achieving great success but it was an important introduction to the possibilities of skating in later years.

We used to go on shopping trips to Stoke and make the occasional visit to 'Daddy's works'. I was a little shy about visiting the works as I didn't like being fussed, called 'duck' or, worst of all, being kissed by the ladies in the decorating room. I was more interested in the gas engine that breathed and spluttered like an angry dragon and had a huge flywheel. There was a long black rope which snaked its way around the workshops over great big pulleys driving the throwing wheels, the turner's lathes and the machine that made the plates. The best place, however, was the packing house as it was full of straw in which you could jump and roll.

Visits to Stoke were *different*. The trip was made by train or charabanc, but rarely by tram as the latter only went as far as Hanford. We caught the train at Trentham Station which was built in the Italian style in keeping with

Trentham Railway Station, c.1920.

Stoke Public Library with its circular windows.

the Hall. From Stoke Station we walked into the town, stopping first by the canal bridge at Wooliscrofts the butcher's shop, which had sawdust on the floor and huge bloody carcasses hanging from the ceiling. In the the main street (Church Street not High Street) was Boots the Chemist where my mother changed her library books. Waites, where I had my hair cut, also sold toys which was exciting – my prize purchase was a clockwork model of *The Majestic*, the flagship of the Cunard Line. Harrison's, a family business, was the general store and sold everything; next to this was Craddock's where we bought our shoes.

Church Street, Stoke-on-Trent.

Then on to Hollins the ironmonger's which had rows and rows of wooden compartments containing nails, screws and all sorts of useful 'things', and where the air was heavy with the pungent smell of oil. Across the road was Bird's the jewellers, run by Mr Bird, a small man with beady eyes and rimless glasses. Next door was the very best shop, Peacock's Penny Bazaar, where my mother sometimes bought me a shiny silver trumpet.

During 1922-1923, Trentham was for the first time linked with Stoke by petrol-driven transport in the form of charabancs, which ran from the road leading to Trentham Gardens. These had canvas hoods and five bench-seats each with a separate door. The conductor collected the fares while standing on the outside running board when the 'chara' was going, holding on to the supports on the canvas roof with his spare arm. When we travelled this way my mother would visit Stoke Public Library which was where the 'chara' stopped. The library, which is still there, was a special building to me because of its circular windows. On the way back from these trips we often stopped for tea at Trentham Gardens before embarking on the long walk home.

Taking the tram to Hanley with mother.

Occasionally we went to Hanley. This meant taking the loop line train to Hanley Station or riding on the tram which went 'ting ting' as it clanked its way up the hill – apparently propelled by the man at the open front with two brass-knobbed handles which he swung from side to side. These expeditions included visits to the cinema where mother exercised a simple form of censorship by putting her hands over our eyes to protect us from the fearsome bits. I remember *Rin Tin Tin*, the Alsatian 'Wonder Dog', who was always jumping over gates or fences to save someone; *Charlie Chaplin* twiddling his walking stick; *The Last Days of Pompeii* as it fell down in all directions, and *Felix the Cat*.

We went on trips by train to Lichfield Cathedral and Tutbury Castle and, of course, London, courtesy of my Aunt Beatrice with whom we stayed at Blackheath. My aunt was a diminutive but formidable spinster who wore black ankle-length dresses and went to church twice each Sunday. She qualified as a doctor in 1905 and had a flourishing practice in which she treated female patients only. We toured London in an open-topped bus on which, for one penny, we could travel for miles. We visited the Tower of London and saw the crown jewels and went to Maskleyne and Cook's theatre which was the centre of 'The Magic Circle' where people disappeared into thin air.

Every summer we took a seaside holiday. In 1921 and 1922 we went to Rhyl where we made sand pies with wooden spades and I lost Wilfred. Wilfred, the rabbit in the *Pip, Squeak and Wilfred* cartoon in the *Daily Mirror*, was the colour of a golden teddy bear and had long ears. I had buried him in the sand and he became a victim of the next high tide. This tragedy led to an ecstatic moment the following Christmas when, protruding from my stocking, were two long ears. Wilfred was back!

My sister Beatrice and me at the seaside with our buckets and wooden spades, Rhyl, 1920.

In 1923 we went to Rhos on Sea near Llandudno. I know that was the year because I was six and I suffered an injury there. We stayed at St. Winifred's Hotel where the path was surfaced with flint chippings. I fell and a flint pierced the middle of my forehead resulting in much blood and a scar which I showed with pride as I retold the gory details. Uncle Harold, Aunt Edith and my cousin, Jo, were also in Llandudno staying at the Rhos Abbey Hotel. Harold, my father's brother, lived in America where he was successful in the oil business. He had come over to visit his father-in-law, a director of Birket, Billington and Newton the brass founders, and a large local company. Jo was ten and could swim – to me she seemed very grown up.

In 1924 we holidayed in Barmouth in a hotel called Myn y Mor. There was a very sandy beach and two-seater go-carts drawn by small ponies which took us for scenic rides. Sometimes we visited a hotel in Arthog for afternoon tea, which meant crossing the estuary over a long wooden bridge which was quite exciting but even more exciting were the ferrets which lived in cages behind the hotel. Other expeditions included going by train and then rowing boat to Shell Island; Harlech Castle was a great adventure as it seemed absolutely huge. Here I suffered another injury when running my hand up the banister of a rough wooden stairway resulting in a large splinter in my palm – I can still feel it. On our first holiday to Barmouth we travelled there and back by train. The second year we returned home by car. This was an open tourer which was just as well as I was carsick but, fortunately, managed to throw up over the side.

Ada Henk as a young girl, second from left, and her family.

Between expeditions and holidays came the time for lessons. We had a governess called Miss Ada Henk, who was tall with curtains of hair on either side of her face. She was the daughter of a continental artist brought over from Germany by Minton's in the 1850s, and lived with her widowed mother in Stoke. Much to our delight, father disgraced himself by composing a little ditty:

Dear Miss Henk was fond of scent
And put it in her hair
When she went into the street
It made rude people stare.

The front room at Glendair became the schoolroom for Beatrice, me and Pamela Irish who came from across the road to join us. We had writing books with rows of pot hooks which we had to copy faithfully to help practice joined-up writing, and we learned about the Vikings. She taught us a great deal more, including drawing and painting, but memory tends to be selective.

Early Schooldays

By the age of eleven I had taken up golf and learned to play bridge

When I was seven we went to Field House School in Stone. This was a fine Georgian building with grounds large enough to accommodate all sporting activities including netball, tennis and cricket. It was run by two Welsh sisters, Miss Annie and Miss Nora Bellis. School work and homework was marked out of ten, with suitable comments when considered necessary. We also had exams marked out of 100. My best achievement was 99/100 for spelling – a mark was deducted because of an alteration in writing the word 'constitution', although I had spelt it correctly. Discipline was strict and teaching was thorough, but I have little recollection of any excitement.

The railway station at Trentham with the extended platform to accommodate the Royal Train.

We travelled to school by train. Mother put us on at Trentham where we sometimes bought a penny bar of Nestle's chocolate from the slot machine on the station platform. Miss Mathews met us at Stone and escorted the gaggle of children to the school. On the half-mile walk to Trentham Station we passed Arthur Ainsworth's farm on our right, then over the canal bridge to the forge where the blacksmith worked with doors open so that you could see the glow of the furnace, hear the clang of hammer on anvil and smell the fitting of a hot shoe to a horse's hoof. Adjoining the smithy was the garage which belonged to Walter Ainsworth, Arthur's brother. Walter was very large and round and a jack-of-all-trades who served us well in later years when he developed his taxi business. He had an extraordinary collection of cars including an Essex Super Six, a Buick, a Morris 12, a Wolsey Limousine (bought from Lord Harrowby) and, finally, a Rolls Royce. As my father never owned a car, Ainsworth's taxis drove us everywhere.

When our leisure activities became more complex 'The Playroom' was erected in the garden. This was a substantial wooden shed measuring some fifteen by twelve feet and housed books, toys and treasures of all kinds including our dapple-grey rocking horse which was the size

Myself, sister Beatrice and father taking tea in the the garden at Glendair.

of a small pony; Gauge 'O' Hornby trains; Meccano; sailing boats; steam-driven motor boats; my clockwork boat, *The Majestic*, and my cinematograph equipment which had superseded my magic lantern and was capable of projecting short lengths of real films. The playroom was heated by an oil stove which led to disaster. In March 1926, while we were having lunch, a billow of smoke passed the window. The oil stove had exploded and our playroom was on fire. Mother opened the shed door to be met by a blast of heat but luckily Mr Oram arrived with our weekly supply of vegetables, and took control of the situation. With a chain of buckets of water the blaze was finally extinguished just before the arrival of the fire engine which was drawn by two black stallions.

In June my mother died of pneumonia. I did not cry because I felt I shouldn't. My Aunt Beatrice rose to the occasion by arriving at Glendair in a London taxi! Everyone wore black for the funeral and all the cottages in the village had their curtains drawn. In just three months I had lost most of my treasures in the fire and then lost my mother. Within two years I had taken up golf and learned to play bridge. I was then eleven years old.

Myself with a 'sea horse' hired from Mr Roberts' shop, 'The Harrods of Borth', 1928.

For a year after my mother's death we were looked after by Constance Aldritt who, under the name of Auntie Consie, broadcasted a children's programme from the local wireless station in Stoke. She was musical and used to play the piano and sing, although I preferred it when she just played the piano. Constance was very young and did her best but left, following a row with my father.

Miss Lasenby then arrived on the scene, brought to Trentham by her Uncle Alwyn in his green, chauffeur-driven Rover. Alwyn Lasenby had known my father since the early 1900s and was a director of Liberty's and W. Moorcroft Ltd. By that time we had two resident maids, Emily and Nancy, so Miss Lasenby's domestic duties were not too arduous. She made up for that by, among other activities, enduring long games of table tennis with me. During that period, we always took our holidays in hotels where the grown-ups changed for dinner in the evening: the Rhos Abbey Hotel, Craigside Hydro, Llandudno, and The Grand Hotel in Borth which was an ambitious project by the Cambrian Railway. The main features of Borth were four miles of sand, a golf course and Mr Roberts' shop which he called 'The Harrods of Borth'. This sold wonderful doughnuts, ideal after a morning bathe, and also hired out inflated rubber horses to play with in the sea. The cottages in the village, which backed on to the sea, had large drainpipes through their foundations to allow the high tide through in the winter. We enjoyed three or four great summer holidays at Borth but I also remember the dejection when dragged off to church on a sunny Sunday morning while everyone else was on the beach.

The garden at Glendair with father and Hazel in deckchairs.

The Boys' High School, Newcastle-under-Lyme.

In the summer term of 1927, I started at Newcastle High School, travelling each way by train, changing at Stoke. On these journeys I was subjected to quite a lot of bullying. Maybe this was because I seemed a bit pi as my father, with the best of intentions, had plied me with such books as *Everlasting Things* by Arthur Mee and *Daily Power,* an anthology of pious quotations. It was a salutary experience which, in the long term, probably did me more good than harm. French was taught phonetically. I persuaded my form master that there was no point in learning it twice. Why spell 'bird' *wazo* when the correct spelling was *oiseau*! He gave me a proper French Grammar instead of one printed in phonetics and commented on my report that I seemed to have an aptitude for languages.

At home in Glendair the garden was landscaped with a pergola supported by pillars of handmade bricks, an arbour built of Horsham stone and a large fountain basin lined with fragments of broken Moorcroft tableware which formed a glittering blue mosaic. We acquired our first wireless, a powerful set which could actually get foreign stations, a large extra room was built on upstairs, furnished more as a recreation room than a bedroom, and the whole house was redecorated regardless of the cost. Father was prospering.

My artwork of the arbour at Glendair, painted while at Holm Leigh Prep School.

Holm Leigh School photograph. Centre left, Captain Noakes, Deputy Headmaster. I am third on the left, middle row, 1929.

My Prep School and Rugby

Biology was my favourite subject as this involved microscopic drawings…

In September 1928, I went as a boarder to my prep school, Holm Leigh in Buxton, which was far more civilised than the High School. In October I received the news that my father had married Miss Lasenby but just how this was conveyed to me I cannot remember except that I had a postcard from Gleneagles where they spent a brief honeymoon playing golf. Miss Lasenby now became Hazel.

Unfortunately, at school I was dubbed a swot by some of the boys as I came top of each form for my first four terms until I reached the sixth form. But I also made good friends with whom I played chess and auction bridge at a sweet a hundred. It was a spartan life, especially in the winter – a face cloth, shaped while wet at bedtime, would become a frozen sculpture by morning if left on the windowsill! My achievements were moderate but I won the school chess championship and succeeded in 'fools mating' the assistant headmaster (checkmate in four moves) in a friendly game. I won the 440 yards championship and have the tiny silver cup I was awarded to this day. A scholastic success was 100% for a geometry exam, achieved by my declaration that question five was impossible. This proved to be the right answer as the question had been incorrectly set. The Assistant Head took a great interest in out-of-school activities and, in 1930, he showed me the first crossword to be published in *The Times*. To this day I can remember 1 down: '*Heraldic gold between Mother and I*' (five letters); answer: '*Maori*.'

At school, my main embarrassment was someone's discovery that I could be made to blush and the words 'Hot Day Moorcroft', especially at mealtimes, would make me turn scarlet. Further embarrassment was caused by the receipt from home of a packet labelled 'Sanitary Straws' – required to avoid the staining of my teeth while taking a tonic with an iron content. A lighter moment came when a school athlete, Moorwood, P., persuaded me, as an escape from boredom, to cut Sunday evening chapel – an exploit which earned us both three of the best in the headmaster's study. There was a highly sophisticated O.T.C. (Officers Training Corps) in which we drilled with wooden rifles. The annual dress parade was performed in white flannels, scarlet blazers and matching caps. Two years went quickly by and I passed my Common Entrance into Rugby.

My tile and a playing card, designed while at prep school.

Holm Leigh Prep School 2nd XI. I am standing on the far right, 2nd November 1929.

O.T.C. inspection parade. Corporal Moorcroft, with wooden rifle and red blazer, following the inspecting officer, 1930.

Myself with Hazel and my father having 'proper' tea on the beach, West Runton, 1933.

N.C.Os of Holm Leigh School, O.T.C. Corporal Moorcroft, far right.

My entrance to Rugby coincided with the opening of Sheriff House so named after Lawrence Sheriff, the founder of Rugby School in 1567. Sheriff House was nicknamed 'the palace' as it had amenities unheard of in the older establishments. It was built at a cost of £56,000 to accommodate fifty-six boys and was featured in *The Architectural Review*. Accommodation included forty-four studies for the fifty-six students, a house library and a private club room for prefects. From the outset I had my own single study which contained a worktable, a wooden chair and an easy chair (the latter to be supplied by the occupant), shelves and cupboard space for storing books and food, a central heating radiator, and a window opening out either on to an inner quadrangle or the outside world.

The dining hall was a high room of fine proportions with oak-beams, oak panelling and large refectory tables, one of which proved ideal for playing table tennis. Meals were served by Crane, the house butler, and his junior assistant. On one occasion Crane entered carrying a wobbly jelly in each hand, after which jelly was known as 'Mae West pudding'. Crane was an institution – he came round the dormitories every morning ringing a handbell and announcing, 'It's harf parst six gentlemen!'

Dormitories were spacious with a window (always open except in severe weather) by every bed. Each dormitory had an adjoining bathroom in which there was one basin with hot and cold running water for every pupil. There was also one spray and one douche shower with cold water only, and you were expected to take a shower every morning. For practical reasons each pair of dormitories was plumbed so that the bathrooms adjoined one another and it was eventually discovered that mugs of water could be thrown through open windows from one bathroom to the next. Battle took place one summer evening. The Housemaster, who happened to be in the library below, was puzzled by drops of water appearing on the window in perfect weather and when he put his head out, received the contents of my mug over his head. Result, three strokes of the cane the following day, but no ill-feelings.

I arrived at Rugby with two serious weaknesses – I could not ride a bicycle and I was unable to swim. I tackled

A group of boys at Rugby walking from one classroom to another. Books, however many, were always carried under the arm – never in a bag or a satchel. I am walking with Pringle Patterson and Ian Miller behind the Master in a gown.

both with great vigour and soon graduated in bicycle-polo, a dangerous game played with a hard ball and hockey sticks. During my first summer term, I not only learned to swim but also managed to dive from the five metre board. The swimming pool measured two hundred by fifty feet, was surrounded by a high wall, and had small lawns for sunbathing. Bathing costumes as such were not worn but at the entrance we were issued with blue-and-white striped cotton drawers known as 'bim-bags'. Each house had its allotted daily swimming times and the pool was opened when the water temperature reached 55°. This was really cold but, with shelter from the wall, it soon warmed up to 70° or more. I swam every day if possible and was a member of the House water-polo team.

Life at Rugby had three directions – learning, sport and general activities. I passed into the next-to-bottom form, and then had to make nine upward moves in twelve terms in order to spend my last year in the sixth form, a privileged status whereby all members automatically became school prefects. Teaching was broadly based. When we were in the year below the School Certificate, our form master told us at the beginning of the term that we were going to cover 2,000 years of history. A hardback notebook was to replace a textbook and, if we did not take proper notes, we would fail the end of term exam. A daunting prospect but our interest was buoyed up by such details as the disgusting habits of Roman emperors. I came top of the form that term after a neck-and-neck struggle with one of my friends, and our form master gave us each a voucher to spend at Over's bookshop 'for working hard'.

The science schools contained extensive laboratories and lecture rooms with separate departments for physics, chemistry and biology. For an exhibition of scientific achievement in 1935, two boys constructed a primitive television apparatus. Significantly, the name of one of the boys was Baird and though I never confirmed a definite connection with the famous scientist, the coincidence seems to be too great. His working partner, Grimston major, was the son of Lord Verulam (no titles at Rugby).

After the School Certificate, teaching separated into three channels – Classics, Modern Languages, and Science and Mathematics. I chose Modern Languages – French, German and Spanish – and, as a pre-condition to learning Spanish, had to gain a credit in School Certificate Latin.

To broaden our outlook we had general science studies which were delivered in lecture form and ranged from Dalton's Atomic Theory, with its explanation of molecular construction, to subjects such as the properties of liquid air,

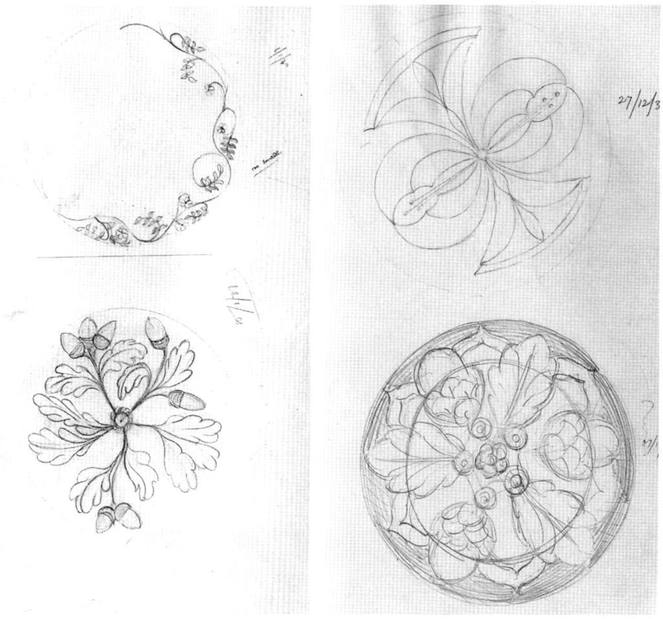

My early designs, aged thirteen.

demonstrated on one occasion by immersing a soft squash ball for a short time, and then smashing it with a hammer, like a piece of porcelain. Biology was my favourite subject as this involved microscopic drawings. An added interest was our biology master, who walked around with a lemur on a lead, which looked rather like him.

Away from our studies, the House library was the centre of communal life. This contained a miscellany of books ranging from the latest *Winnie the Pooh* by A.A. Milne, received, I may say, with great acclaim, to an 1875 edition of the *Encyclopaedia Britannica* which contained no less than 135 pages on chess. Newspapers were delivered daily including *The Times* and we became keen followers of its crossword. I cherish the memory of an exchange of letters in *The Times* about its crossword which I quote in approximate detail:

From Sir Austin Chamberlain (a famous old Rugbeian):
'The Editor of The Times
Dear Sir, I derive great pleasure from your crossword which I do daily in forty minutes. Yours faithfully etc.'

Two days later:
'The Editor of The Times
Dear Sir, I also enjoy your crossword which I normally complete in the time it rakes to boil an egg.
Yours faithfully, The Provost of Eton'

Two days later:
'The Editor of the Times
Dear Sir, With reference to the letter from the Provost of Eton about your crossword, I presume he likes his eggs very hardboiled! Yours faithfully, Austin Chamberlain'

The school was divided into eleven Houses and, apart from school teams, all sports were fiercely contested at House level. I did not make any of the school teams but played for my House at rugby football, hockey, table tennis, water polo and on the odd occasion, cricket, for which I lacked enthusiasm and, whenever possible, abandoned in favour of tennis. In addition to tennis we played a lot of squash. An unofficial game was 'quad hockey' which we played four- or five-a-side on an asphalt yard at the back of our house – fast, furious, but surprisingly free from injury. After watching an inter-school rugby match, we had to go for a three-mile run; if matches were cancelled because of bad weather the run was extended to five miles. I usually made good time as I liked to be among the first back for a hot shower.

We were free to roam the countryside within a wide radius, either on foot or by bicycle. A favourite haunt in the summer was an oxbow bend in a local stream where we swam, sunbathed and savoured illicit cigarettes. My friend, Peter Abbott, was a dedicated bug-collector and collected all but about six of the 180 varieties of bumble bee native to the British Isles. He also succeeded in transferring a fully functioning wasps' nest into his study, and hung the ovoid paper-like construction from a string in the window, much to the interest of the science staff. In 1934 the new Shakespeare Theatre at Stratford-upon-Avon was completed and our House Tutor took a small party to see the building. After a brief tour we were left to our own devices and spent the rest of the day in a punt on the river. I took a photograph of Peter Abbott smoking a pipe in an apparently idyllic situation but, when I showed this to him at a reunion fifty years later, he admitted that, at the time, he had felt slightly sick.

Illicit bathing in a stream – Henry Moyers and I balance precariously on a floating log.

My schoolfriend, Peter Abbott, in a punt on the Avon at Stratford, 1934.

In the summer term of 1935 I spent much of my time swimming and playing tennis but managed in between times to get my Higher School Certificate in French, German and English. As my German tutor used to say if we looked bored, '*alles kommt zu ende*' – 'everything comes to an end' – and so, eventually, do schooldays. I was informed that there would be a place for me at Cambridge if I wished to take it. Shrewdly, my father left me to make the decision whether to go to university or to start work at the factory. As neither his health nor his finances were in very good shape, I decided on the latter. As events turned out this was to be crucial to the survival of Moorcroft Pottery to the present day.

A pre-war aerial photograph of the factory showing the proximity to the railway. The platform of Cobridge Station can just be seen on the right. On the left of the factory is the cooper's yard where all our casks were made for export packing.

My Working Life Begins

I kept a daily diary...with references to golf, bridge and the wireless...

School days were over and it was time for growing-up. My knowledge of 'life' was very limited; in English the letters s-e-x commonly appeared only in the two counties, Essex and Sussex. My Housemaster had obviously been too embarrassed by a private school leavers' talk in his study to get down to the facts of life, while my father would only occasionally refer darkly to the importance of 'avoiding immorality'.

I began work at the factory on Monday 30th September 1935. I had no specific duties but was expected to observe the general progress of production in the factory for which I received no pay but lived well, travelling to work by a first-class railway season ticket and enjoying lunch every day at the Grand Hotel in Hanley. My father's tailor, Jennings of Burslem, supplied me with dinner jacket, white tie and tails for dances, sports jacket and the occasional suit and I bought ready-made slacks. As a primitive form of market research, I bought a pair of socks costing 2s 6d from six different shops in Hanley, then patronised the one which gave me the best service. Despite my lack of a regular income, I kept a meticulous account of my expenditure which I balanced every month.

I kept a daily diary. This reflected a relatively mundane existence with references to golf, bridge and the wireless. One of my favourite programmes was the B.B.C. Dance Orchestra conducted by Henry Hall who succeeded Jack Payne, its conductor from the early days. A programme of gramophone records was presented by Christopher Stone who, when introducing each record, also announced all the details from its label. There were also symphony concerts which included the audience's prolonged applause after each performance. The B.B.C. did not broadcast dance music on Sundays but this could be heard on Radio Luxembourg, one of the pioneers of commercial broadcasting. Further afield, I listened to news programmes from Berlin, *The Berliner Nachrichtungsdienst*, and to Radio Roma during a brief attempt to learn Italian.

My father encouraged me to play golf by giving me the price of a new ball and a caddie each time there was a competition, and I think he took pride in my successes on the course. He played golf every Saturday afternoon often with Tom and Fred Wild who owned the factory which made Royal Albert china, and sometimes played with me on midweek evenings. He also played bridge. On returning home from work he would have a cup of tea then set off to the golf club for a quick rubber often with Sir Ernest Johnson, of Johnson Brothers the earthenware manufacturers, and Ted Hewitt the managing director of Copelands. This nearly always lasted a lot longer than expected, making him late for our evening meal which was served at 7.30 precisely. This was condoned by our cook, Nellie, in whose eyes he could no wrong, but was frowned upon by Hazel.

In these days before television, reading was an important pastime. While at school we had a play-reading society for which I had acquired omnibus editions of the plays of John Galsworthy, Noel Coward and George Bernard Shaw. The part I remember reading with most satisfaction was that of Professor Higgins in *Pygmalion*. Over a period of years I found a wealth of light reading by authors including Edgar Wallace, E. Phillips Oppenheim, P.G. Wodehouse, Agatha Christie, Dorothy Sayers, Marjorie Allingham, J.B. Priestley, Vicki Baum, and Lin Yutang in whose books about China I had a special interest. In addition to English novels, I maintained a keen interest in foreign languages as a compensation for missing university studies, and read German, French and Spanish books which I bought new and second-hand from Foyles Bookshop in London. My choice of books tended to be on the light side as I was interested more in the use of language rather than the structure of classical literature, and I often wrote my diary in Spanish to practice using simple phrases. I also bought foreign newspapers such as *Le Monde* and *L'Intransigeant* from France, and the *Berliner Illustrierte Zeitung* and the *Kölnische Illustrierte Zeitung* from Germany. I still have a copy of the latter illustrating the famous 1936 Olympic Games which were so ruthlessly exploited for Nazi propaganda. I cherish the memory of a quotation from a Spanish novel, the name of which escapes me; *'Los Buenos pintores imitan la natualeza, los males lo vomitan'* – 'The good painters imitate nature, the bad ones vomit it.' The idea of bad painters vomiting nature has always appealed to me!

Starting work was a big step but sporting activities remained very important to me and I was pleased to be invited to join the North Staffordshire Hockey Club. There was also a squash court at Lawton Hall Hotel, a few miles from home, and I had some greatly appreciated opponents who owned cars and were good enough to drive me there. When the tennis season came around, I was very fortunate to have three hospitable friends, Rex Alcock, David Dickson and Anthony Allardice, all of whom had tennis courts at home.

In December 1935 I took a day trip to London – an intriguing outing for a nineteen-year-old. I recorded in my diary:

> '12th December. Went up to London on 7.40. Went to the Royal Academy to see the Chinese Exhibition, which was remarkably good. Lunched at Fortnum and Masons with Lady Harcourt Smith and Lady Wolston, a most enjoyable and vivacious lunch. Lady W. was perfectly charming. Went on to St. James' Palace and went in through the corner yard and in by the diplomatic entrance. We were ushered round by commissionaires and were let behind all the barriers, which held back the crowd.' (Just what we were looking at is not recorded.)

That year we spent Christmas at Craigside Hydro in Llandudno, which had covered tennis courts built on an imposing scale at the turn of the century, and a ballroom in which there was dancing every evening. I played in a tennis tournament on Christmas day and an entry in my diary reads:

> '28th December. Another tennis tournament. Had a much nicer partner and played much better. Danced till 1.00am with Molly and made friends with Connie despite her former black looks. Got on very well. Waltzed till I could hardly stand with C.'

My father excelled himself on this occasion. He had been in poor health for several months and, in addition to a warning against indulgence in nicotine and alcohol, he set off with a small case filled with medication. On our return home, his doctor commented on the great improvement brought about by his short break. My father said he did indeed feel much better. He realised that his system needed a change in treatment as well as a change of air. As he never had indulged heavily in smoking or drinking, he had taken each evening a glass of sherry before dinner, wine with his meal and a cigar and liqueur afterwards, leaving the case of medication untouched!

We returned to Craigside for Christmas 1936. Connie was there again, and she played a large part in my enjoyment. My diary has lengthy details, all written in Spanish, and Connie, referred to as 'Conita', features daily supported by other young people, Pamela, Joan and Gordon. During the day we played tennis, table tennis, deck tennis and bridge, and I danced as much as possible with Connie in the evenings. It was a happy interlude but afterwards we went our separate ways, never to meet again.

Earlier that same year we took our summer holiday in Hunstanton where we met the West Russell family – father, son (a Rugbeian), and two daughters, Marion and Lois. I became very good friends with Lois and was invited to stay at their London home in Hamilton Terrace the following year. This visit to London in 1937 was a great success and had all the activities of a house party including a special dance at the Lyceum Club, a sumptuous Victorian mansion in Curzon Street. My partner for the evening was fellow guest, Mew Wightman from Edinburgh, who was attractive, vivacious and excellent company. We spent much of the evening reclining on a large settee drinking gin and lime and smoking Abdullah Egyptian cigarettes with gold tips, which were much appreciated.

During my early working days I had difficulty in coming to grips with the day-to-day running of the factory which seemed to be freewheeling rather than actively driven. Although my father needed help, he was reluctant to delegate any of his activities and I learned by observation rather than instruction. Every Monday morning I watched the bottle-oven being 'drawn' by a team of men inside, passing down the saggars to be emptied by the women on the ground. In the course of firing, pieces were sometimes damaged through the fault of the placer who put them into the saggars. As soon as the oven was empty I used to look around inside, before these could be conveniently disposed of. Results from the glost oven were unpredictable and this often led to explosive rows between my father and the fireman – in the interests of my father's health, I learned to pre-empt these by a more diplomatic approach.

However, as the local accent and dialect was still in everyday use, there were difficulties of communication with the work people. The ladders used inside the bottle-ovens were the *'big oss'* and the *'little oss'*. *'Oss'* being spelt horse, and it was a long time before I discovered the *'esshole'* was spelt 'ash hole'. Then there was the expression *'aze gone wom'* – 'he has gone home' – from which also came the phrase *'it's time to wom it'*. Eventually, I found a key to a whole vocabulary of pronunciations by observing the fact that, when walking from point A to point B in a town, one went *'street down the straight'* not 'straight down the street'. This interchange of 'a' and 'e' sounds occurred time and again. I have a vivid memory of a brief interlude on Cobridge railway station. On the platform a teenage boy and his attractive girlfriend were waiting for the train. There was an exchange of badinage between the boy and the lad from the ticket office, who was obviously envious. As the train came in sight he said, *'Years trine weesht breek darn weelt theyt ont'* which translated into, 'Here is the train, I wish it would break down while thou art on it'. The girl said sweetly, 'Isn't his elocution strange.' This use of the second person singular was quite common, appearing frequently in *'thar costner'* – 'thou canst not'.

My uncle, Harold Moorcroft, enjoying his retirement at Walton-on-the-Hill.

In May 1936, I spent a weekend with my Uncle Harold, Aunt Edith and cousin Josephine at their house near Reigate, bought when they returned from America in the late 1920s. We played golf each day at Walton Heath. Jo, who looked like Jessie Mathews, played off a handicap of four. She drove a Chrysler Convertible with a white bull terrier as a passenger. Jo was and is, very good company.

Artwork was my father's sole prerogative and the few pieces which I managed to design bore his signature. These included a vase, designed while I was still at school as part of a project for the Jubilee of King George V and Queen Mary. On the 7th December I noted in my diary, 'D. did not come to the works. Sketched a decorative swallow on to a pot in the morning.' I did the drawing on a rough thrown *Natural Pottery* vase and followed it up with a pelican – while the cat's away! My next effort was a bantam or fighting cock which I put on to a large spherical vase. This was finished in rich *flambé* colours and is illustrated in *Moorcroft – A Guide to Moorcroft Pottery 1897-1993* by Paul Atterbury, p129. In 1937, the Duchess of Gloucester visited our stand at the B.I.F. (British Industries Fair) and the only piece she bought was a powder-box which I had designed with a pink *Tiger Lily* on a white background. No reference was made to me as the designer although I was present at the time. I was disappointed but passed no comment as I had learned to take my father's possessive attitude for granted. He *was* Moorcroft.

In February each year the B.I.F. was held in London over a period of two weeks. A trade exhibition to promote exports, it had been staged annually since 1915 and attracted a number of important visitors, including royalty. For the two weeks of the Fair we stayed at the De Vere Hotel in Kensington, a highly respectable establishment patronised by the Duke of Beaufort and a number of resident ladies who, on Sundays, received their expectant nephews for afternoon tea. We had a very imposing exhibition stand made in oak by Liberty and Co. who stored it in their cellars during the year and erected it and dismantled it for the period of the Fair, sending their French polisher to add the finishing touches. Like all trade fairs the B.I.F. represented long hours in anticipation of the vital orders, especially for the junior exhibitor. There were, however, brighter moments over the years that I can best recall by quoting from my diaries:

> '20th February 1936. Father had a bad cold and did not come to Olympia early. Mrs Claude Taylor (imposing wife of the director of the B.I.F.) came in about 10.00 and introduced me to Herr Berner the leader of a party of a dozen Germans from their embassy. I hoped to use my knowledge of German but most of them spoke English.' (My first week.)
>
> '23rd February 1937. At 10.00 Queen Mary and the Duchess of Gloucester came to see us. Queen Mary came first and the minute she came to the stand she took my father's hand and said, "Did you think I was not going to come! On Tuesday there was not time and we were very tired."' (Translated from my original entry written in Spanish.)

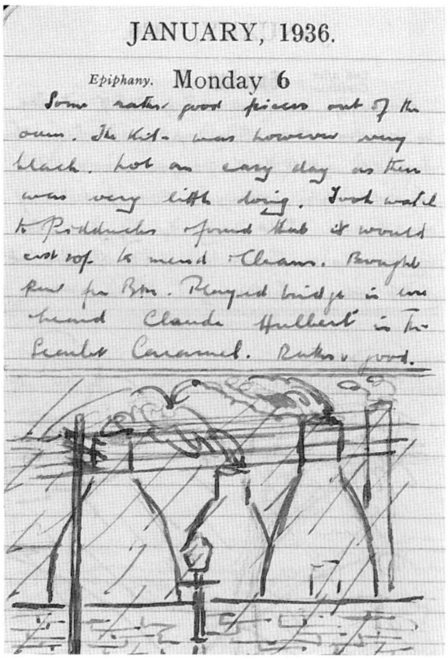
JANUARY, 1936.
Epiphany. Monday 6

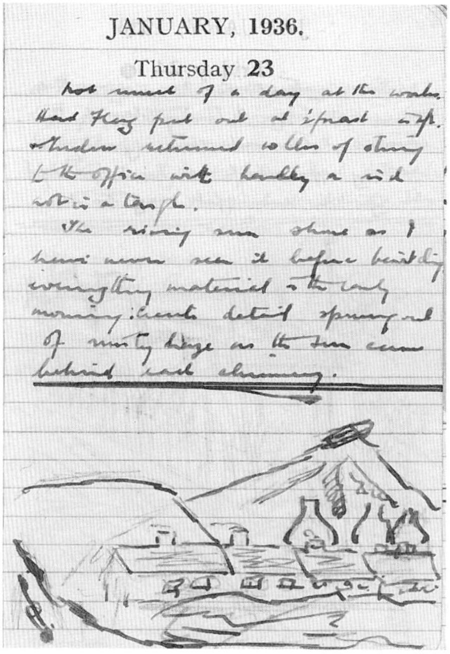
JANUARY, 1936.
Thursday 23

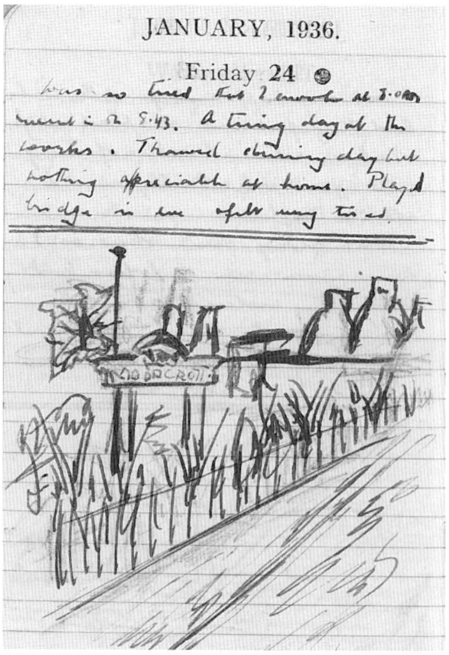
JANUARY, 1936.
Friday 24

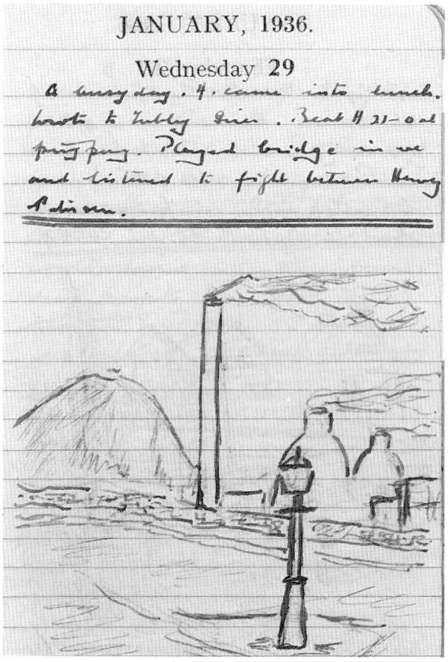
JANUARY, 1936.
Wednesday 29

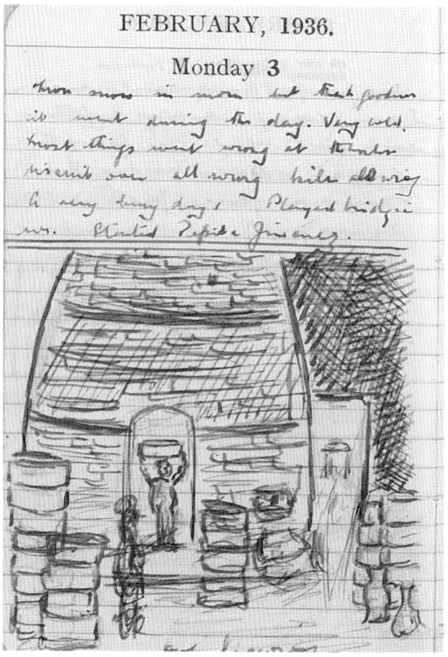
FEBRUARY, 1936.
Monday 3

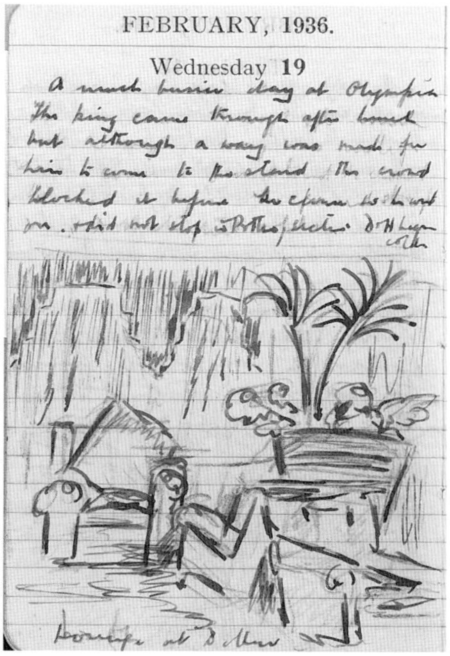
FEBRUARY, 1936.
Wednesday 19

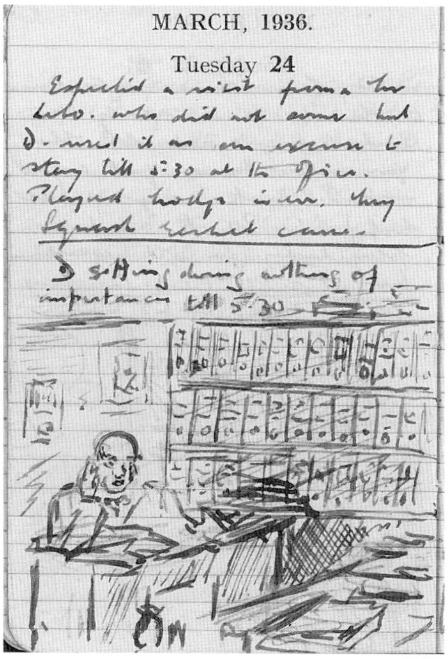
MARCH, 1936.
Tuesday 24

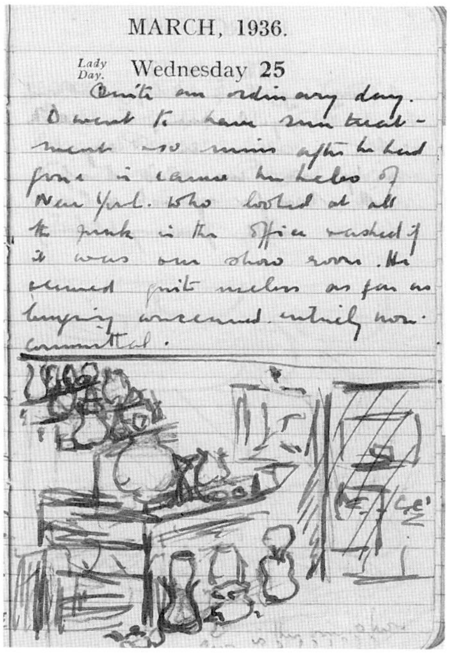
MARCH, 1936.
Lady Day. Wednesday 25

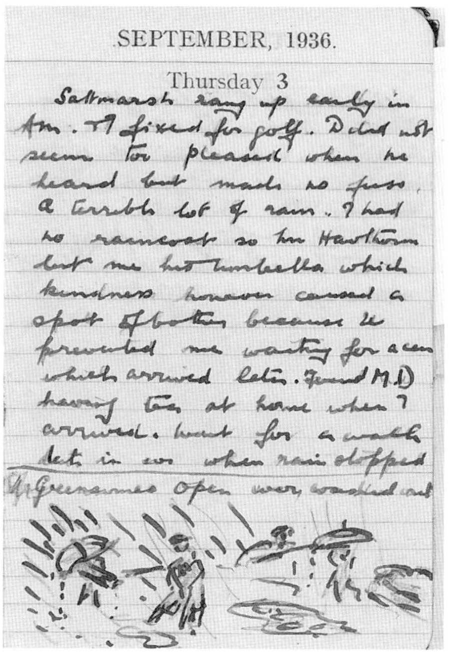
SEPTEMBER, 1936.
Thursday 3

'22nd February 1937. Ramsey MacDonald came in with Sir Edward Crowe who introduced him to my father and then to me. He talked mainly to my father but bade me a friendly goodbye as he left.' (Again translated.)

'24th February 1938. A day of Royal visits. Queen Mary came as usual and was very handsome in a rich tone of purple. Pa got off with the Dowager Countess of Airlie on the grounds of their meeting in 1918. The old bird had to be dragged off the stand by an official. General grievance abroad because the Queen demanded the cheapest of everything she bought.'

'25th February 1938. A complete dearth of business in almost every section of Olympia. A visit from Haile Selassie during the afternoon caused a brief stir of interest. Went along for coffee with Sir Cecil and Lady Harcourt Smith after supper. Lady H.S. insisted on playing rummy but gave up in despair after trying to teach Pa. She was in fits of laughter hearing two men declaim the morals of every side of modern life in the official world and other quarters.'

'21st February 1939. A visit from Queen Mary and a photograph of her on the stand were the features of the morning. Talked to the Duke of Kent who reminded me of his wedding present.' (The photograph referred to is now hanging in the factory museum.)

Although we worked for six days each week, the evenings and Sundays were free and I made the most of what London had to offer. I bought clothes at Simpsons of Piccadilly and Lillywhites, and had my hair cut at Austin Reed's in Regent Street who had Moorcroft vases in *Autumn Leaves flambé* adapted to contain their hair lotions. On Sundays I walked in the parks or went skating with friends on the Westminster Ice Rink. At the cinema I saw the latest films with my favourite stars, Ginger Rogers and Jessie Matthews and, on a more demanding level, French and German films at the Berkeley and Studio One. I usually managed to make at least one visit to the theatre where I enjoyed the lighter side of entertainment and I quote some highlights from my diaries:

'22nd February 1936. Had lunch with Aunt Ethel at the De Vere and went with her to see *Follow the Sun* at the Adelphi.' (This was a Charles B. Cochran revue supported by his famous chorus girls.)

'13th February 1937. Went with my cousin Francisca (known to the family as Budge) to see Jack Buchanan and Elsie Randolph in *This'll Make you Whistle* at Daly's Theatre.'

'21st February 1939. Dashed off at 7.15 to Budge's flat for supper then went on to see Diana Wynward, Rex Harrison and Anton Walbrook in *Design for Living*. They put across Noel Coward's exquisite dialogue perfectly.'

'28th February 1939. Left the fair early and made a rapid change to meet Pat just after 7.00. She was in a dark blue décolleté dress with white spots and looked ravishing. We took supper together at the De Vere then went to the Queen's Theatre to see *Dear Octopus* with John Gielgud and Marie Tempest.'

In *Dear Octopus*, the children whispered the words 'district nurse' furtively, because of the link to childbirth. Twenty years later my eight- and ten-year-old daughters came home from school sniggering about 'L.C.L.' (*Lady Chatterley's Lover*) which, because of its use of four-letter words and descriptions of sexual behaviour, became the subject of much public argument. *Plus ça change, plus c'est la même chose!*

Over a period of years I discovered the joy of ballet and for me the blend of music, movement and colour was beyond description. I will not attempt to recount precise details but I saw many of the leading dancers including Margot Fonteyn, Moira Shearer, Beryl Grey, Robert Helpmann and Rudolf Nuryev.

1937 was coronation year for King George VI and Queen Elizabeth. Commemorative ware has always had a place in the pottery industry and this was no exception. We had already produced a group of tankards and tobacco jars for the anticipated coronation of King Edward VIII, which we had disposed of by doubling the price and selling them to Harrods. We made a similar range for George VI with the addition of a covered cigarette jar and some ashtrays.

The Coronation was commemorated at the Golf Club by the Coronation Cup, an enormous silver trophy made especially for the occasion. The competition was played over two rounds and I tied with a scratch golfer, Ken McKee. The following week we were sent out for an eighteen-hole replay and, again, we tied. To avoid further delay we were asked to play eighteen holes after tea and I lost by one shot on the last green. According to my diary 'There was a huge gathering round the eighteenth green who showered me with congratulations and commiserations.' This marathon makes a good case for 'sudden death' as played today. During the same year, two squash courts were built at the Golf Club and I played several times a week. To quench the players' thirst, the club sold beer throughout the winter – hitherto it had not been sold between October and March. A game of squash, a hot shower, and a pint of ale was a perfect tonic after a day's work.

In August 1937 we went to Jersey for our summer holiday, a six-hour crossing from Weymouth. On arrival at the Hotel Victor Hugo, I hastily changed into my dinner jacket for the evening meal only to find that everyone else was in slacks and open-necked shirts. This did me no harm however, as I met some really attractive girls with whom I enjoyed table tennis, lawn tennis and various escapades. For many years my father expressed the wish that I should not smoke until I was twenty-one (a wish that I observed within reason). When drinking coffee after our evening meal, he extracted a cigarette from his gold case and then offered me one which I accepted without comment other than a simple 'thank you'. I have smoked ever since.

After a week my holiday was cut short owing to administrative problems at the factory. To avoid the lengthy journey by sea I flew from Jersey to Southampton which was quite exciting. The plane had two propellors and fourteen seats. It took nearly five minutes to start the second propeller and we flew into Southampton dropping like a stone as we passed through air pockets. I informed the family of my safe arrival with a telegram in Spanish,

Cecily Miller, sister of my schoolfriend Ian, and myself at 2am in the bar of the Grand Hotel Kurhaus, Lenzerheide.

The ski class, Lenzerheide, January 1937. I am standing second from left.

'*Todo se ha pasado deleitosamente*'. The girl at the desk asked if this was in code, as codes carried an extra charge! The air fare was £1 17s 6d. A substantial compensation for this loss of my holiday time came in the form of a fortnight's skiing in Switzerland over the New Year. I was invited to join a mixed party of about sixteen, including some of my best school-friends. We stayed at the Grand Hotel Kurhaus, Lenzerheide, about fifteen miles from St. Moritz and the total cost of the trip was £32 19s 4d. We used wooden skis to which we attached sealskins in order to grip the snow when climbing beyond the limit of the funicular. An entry in my 1938 diary reads as follows:

'Average day at the Kurhaus:

9.00am	Turn over in bed and open one eye
9.20am	Roll out of bed
9.55am	Order lunch and then breakfast (10 being the last hour for lunches – penalty 1 franc)
10.30am	Think about starting
10.45am	Ditto
11.00am	Set off somewhere, probably the Funi
11.00-1.00pm	High speed skiing and still higher speed falling
1.15pm	A huge lunch anywhere
2.15pm	More high speed
4.00pm	Back to tea
4.15pm	A huge tea with cherry jam rolls and chocolate
4.30-5pm	Cigarettes, music and memories
5.15-7.15pm	Bridge for love or 10 cents
8.00pm	Dinner
9.00pm	Dancing
10-11-12-1-2	Ditto
3-4-5	Ditto
4.00-9.00am	Sleep and how.'

My Twenty-First Birthday

In the summer I bought a Standard Super Six Saloon for £44...

February 1938 heralded my twenty-first birthday and payment of a salary by the company. This was offered as either £4 per week or £200 per year. I politely pointed out that £4 a week was, in fact, £208 a year, and got it. I celebrated my birthday while in London for the B.I.F. with a small dinner party at the Savoy Hotel consisting of my sister, Beatrice, a golfing friend, Gilbert Loughnan, and my special friend, Lois, described in my diary as 'charming as she could be in white with a silver fox cape'. We had a floor-side table in the ballroom. One wall consisted entirely of mirrors and for the cabaret, the dance floor rose up to table height on hydraulics, which was extremely impressive. We ate a wonderful meal and drank Gin Fizz which had been the 'in' drink when we were in Switzerland. We danced to the music of Carol Gibbons and his Savoy Orpheans, and Geraldo, whose bands interchanged on a revolving stage at the end of the ballroom. I made the most of my time with Lois, leaving Gilbert to dance with my sister whenever possible.

During the past year I had been too preoccupied or just ignorant to notice any significant change in my stepmother, Hazel. On the 22nd February, when staying at the De Vere Hotel during the B.I..F., I received a letter from her telling me that she was expecting a baby the following month. I refrained from comment. My brother, John, was born on the 29th March 1938 and an entry in my diary the following day was more explicit:

> '30th March. Slept infernally badly. Had Dad on one side snoring like a rhinoceros with most insistent regularity and the baby crying on the other side of the passage. HELL.' (There were twin beds in my room.)

My dismay over the arrival of John was short-lived and life soon returned to normal. Increased activity at the factory, plenty of golf and a couple of highly entertaining dances put things in the right perspective.

My first car – a Standard Super Six, bought for £44 in 1938.

My second car – a Flying Standard, £70, October 1939.

My third car – a Talbot 65 Saloon which gave sterling service to the Home Guard by carrying a machine gun section.

Lanchester Coupe with Albert Salmon's body, bought for 99 guineas, 1942.

My first post-war car – an SS 1934 Continental Saloon.

A big step forward in design – a Rover 75, 1951.

My Ford Convertible with Liz at the wheel and a full complement of passengers, 1958.

In the 1930s, dances played an important part in social life and formal dress was the order of the day with white tie and tails for the men and long evening gowns for the girls. On occasions there were even programme dances which meant that on arrival, each male guest was presented with a numbered list of the dances on a deckle-edged card with a small pencil attached by a silk cord with which to enter the name of each partner through the evening. Then began the pursuit of the most nubile females before they were all booked. A leading function in the social calendar was a New Year's Eve dance staged each year by Adolf Wenger at his home, Trentham Priory. Adolf, with his brothers, Henry and Theodore, owned Wenger's colour works at Etruria, which was a highly successful business, manufacturing colours and materials for the ceramic and allied industries. Adolf was an imposing figure with a dark moustache and a pointed beard. In winter he might be seen occasionally wearing a cape and a Tyrolean hat, in keeping with his Swiss origins. The Priory stood in extensive grounds and each summer a garden party took place which was by far the largest of the season. This was a target for ladies of 'good works' to make their mark in local society. It was a large, nineteenth-century house with the traditional baize door closing off the servants' quarters. It also had a ballroom, which was an essential feature for the annual dance.

My father and Adolf were old friends and on Sundays we were often invited to the Priory for afternoon tea. On one occasion, we were sitting as usual in the drawing room when the butler entered and walked around squirting what looked like fly spray, but proved to be an anti-infection device which Adolf had seen used in the local cinema to which, somewhat paradoxically, he took his wife for entertainment. To maintain his status as the squire, Adolf was a regular churchgoer and walked the short distance from the Priory to the church, smoking a large cigar. He was dissuaded from leaving this in the church porch to re-light after the service, following a discreet reference to the habit in the parish magazine.

Photograph from the train: air raid shelters for the Shelton Steel Works under construction, before being covered by 'shraff' from the coal mine, 1938.

Jean and I recline on a pedestal, Trentham Swimming Pool, 1939.

My attempts to learn the piano were abandoned after my first year at Rugby, but we received excellent lectures on the structure of orchestral music backed up by concerts given by the Birmingham Symphony Orchestra. This enabled me to enjoy many performances at the Victoria Hall in Hanley, which had very fine acoustics and attracted the leading musicians of the day. I had the privilege of attending concerts conducted by Sir John Barbirolli, Sir Thomas Beecham, Adrian Boult, Anatole Fistoulari, Sir Malcolm Sargent and Sir Henry Wood. On one occasion when Sir Henry was conducting, a solitary clap was heard at the end of the first movement – the great man turned round on the podium and glared. Silence was total.

For my twenty-first birthday, my father had given me £50 with which to buy a car. In the summer I bought a Standard Super Six Saloon for £44, the possession of which opened new horizons. In the past I had been very fortunate in receiving lifts from friendly car-owners, but it is difficult to make progress with a girlfriend in other people's vehicles and, by now, I had met Jean who was a classic 'dumb blonde' but gorgeous with it. During the next two years she and I spent many happy hours on the golf course, in the swimming pool at Trentham Gardens, at the cinema, and making the social rounds of dances.

By 1938 business at the factory was beginning to improve. My personal ambition was to get the turnover up to £10,000 a year which would give us a chance of making a profit. My diary records a visit from Max Daum of New York which was far more significant than we realised at the time. In 1937 we had restarted our lamp base business in the United States with the Crest Company of Chicago, but they only bought specialised decorations with colours such as oxblood and plain celadon. Max Daum bought our regular decorations and laid the foundation for the business with other distributors which kept us going during the Second World War. In September there were already rumblings of war which are reflected in these entries from my diary:

'Monday 26th. Listened to Hitler's speech from the Sportpalast in Berlin. An hour and a quarter of it.

Understood most of it. The finest statement of a case any barrister could have made, but no compromise.'

'Wednesday 28th. News at 5.00pm came through of conference between Chamberlain, Hitler, Mussolini and Daladier, a vast relief.'

'Friday 30th. Everything was lit up by the news of peace. The Munich conference was a success. Heard Chamberlain's arrival in London and was fired with the wild enthusiasm of the rain-soaked crowds.'

It would not be long before the same crowds blamed Chamberlain for weakness and appeasement. At the end of 1938 another skiing party was arranged with the same group as in the previous year. This time we went to Adelboden in the Bernese Oberland. In the interest of economy (£7 return fare) we made the four hour sea-crossing from Newhaven to Dieppe and then by overnight train, with wooden seats, to Switzerland. As we left England there was snow right down to the waterfront at Newhaven. We spent Christmas in Adelboden and had lunch on Christmas Day sitting in the sun at 6,000 feet. The Grand Hotel staged an ice gala, after which we skated by moonlight with snowclad peaks rising to 3,000 feet all around us.

Father, Courtney Haddock, the buyer for Woodward's Stores, Vancouver, and myself outside the factory, 1939.

Peace in the Alps. My photograph taken on reaching the top of the Hahnemoos Pass, Adelboden, 1st January 1939.

The New Year began peacefully enough for me on the ski slopes of Switzerland. My diary records the end of my holiday on Sunday 8th January with a rough crossing from Dieppe to Newhaven, which my friends Ian, Gerry and I coped with by having a four-course lunch and a glass of beer in the dining saloon before finding a place on the top deck which was sheltered from the high wind. On arriving in London I decided against pushing on home and spent the night in Ian's flat. The following morning I missed the early train to Stoke owing to a dearth of taxis, and decided to stay in town to make a tour of the London stores as a late appearance at the works would have been of little use. I visited Heals, Maples, John Lewis, Selfridges, Marshall & Snelgove, Peter Jones, and Fortnum & Mason. At Maples, I was informed that there was very little Moorcroft about now. The company was, they thought, making tiles. Decorated Moorcroft had become almost unrecognised in London. Our *Powder Blue Tableware*, which appealed to quite a different public, was stocked by the Army & Navy Stores, Liberty and John Lewis, and had been the mainstay of our sales in the home-market. Our improved business came almost entirely from abroad, mainly North America.

In May 1939, the factory was visited by Marcel Goldscheider of Vienna, a member of the family famous for their ceramic figures, especially in the 1930s, depicting ladies of fashion. His Jewish grandfather had been turned out of Austria with 1,000 marks and no front teeth, these having been knocked out during a Nazi dispute. It was, he told us, the end of a five-hundred year family connection with ceramics in Czechoslovakia and Vienna.

The summer passed uneventfully with golf, tennis and swimming in my leisure hours. I was invited to join a small party for a week's holiday at the Cliff Hotel, Trearddur Bay, Anglesey, but declined as I was saving up for a skiing trip in the winter. As August advanced, the situation in Europe deteriorated and the following comments are from my diary in the final days before the war:

'Monday 21st August. Bloody war scares put a bit of a pall over things.'

'Tuesday 22nd. A pretty piggish sort of day with no improvement in European news.'

'Thursday 24th. News steadily blacker.'

'Wednesday 30th. Political spheres hanging by very narrow threads.'

'Friday 1st September. Germany marched into Poland. News came in during the morning. A sort of lull followed. Tomorrow's golf match was cancelled.'

'Sunday 2nd. Still no war news. D. very adamant about my carrying on at the works. The idea seems rather awful to me unless some home service crops up alongside.'

My father on the ice at Trentham Lake for the first time since 1896.

I capture Cecily Bellamy, chasing her shadow in the morning sun.

Pottery people, John Aynsley and Margot Wenger.

Declaration of war, 11am on the 3rd September 1939. At the golf club, Ken Wild and Charlie Wood look grave as we listen to the announcement by the Prime Minister, Neville Chamberlain, that we have declared war on Germany.

War is Declared

I was pleased to list golf, hockey, tennis, squash, badminton, table tennis, skating, skiing and swimming...Great assets for intelligence work!

On Sunday the 3rd of September we interrupted our morning round of golf in order to hear an announcement by the Prime Minister, Neville Chamberlain. He solemnly stated that as from 11.00am we were at war with Germany. Having a camera in my pocket I photographed the proceedings, then we finished the round. I was above the age of immediate call-up and my father was adamant about my carrying on at the works. Loyalty to him eased my conscience over not being an 'heroic' volunteer. A number of factories were closed, but we were allowed to continue production as exports were vital to the economy, and we had War Office contracts for making items such as hospital inhalers and toothbrush holders 'officers for the use of', which had remained on the official list since the First World War.

January 1940 was extremely cold and there was skating for over a week on Trentham Lake. War or no war, this was a social occasion with everyone turning out, either on skates or as spectators. My father donned skates for the first time in forty years and a diminutive John made an appearance on the ice.

During this year I met Margaret who had come from London to Trentham Gardens, because of the evacuation of the Central Clearing House of Banks. Margaret had worked for the fashion house of Worth in London, an experience which added to her natural charm and sophistication. She had a great gift for conversation, and taught me that walking in the rain in the right company could be more rewarding than an expensive night out.

Life as a civilian began to make me feel like a second-class citizen and the formation of the L.D.V. (Local Defence Volunteers), which later became the Home Guard, was a great relief. In the early days of the L.D.V., before we even had uniforms, my section commander was Alf Sherwin, a director of H. & R. Johnsons, an international tile company. At the end of a term of duty, we were relieved by another section led by a little man who managed a grocer's shop and barked orders at his men like a sergeant major. Alf showed the contrast in leadership and turned to us and asked, with an exaggerated drawl, 'Everyone ready? Shoulder arms chaps!'

One of our duties was to man a traffic control point in Strongford Bridge on the main road to Stafford, and our headquarters was the dairy house of a nearby farm. One summer evening we were on duty at 6.00pm as usual, and I was detailed to drive back to Trentham to pick up up someone who was working late. I returned after half-an-hour to find the door was locked and bolted. From inside came the voice of my section commander, Kenneth Bailey, demanding a password. As he had known me since childhood and having no knowledge of any password, I replied with the first word which came to mind – 'bollocks'. Kenneth showed strong disapproval but took no disciplinary action. A week or so later, on a Sunday morning exercise, Jack Noke, the Art Director of

Doultons and a senior Home Guard officer, spotted me and asked quietly, 'Any new passwords lately?' News had obviously travelled! There were many 'characters' in the Home Guard and one I remember with affection was our local plumber, Reg Smith, who had a large notice board outside his house which read, R. Smith, R.P. and A.S.W.P.B., which stood for Registered Plumber and Associate of the Staffordshire Potteries Water Board. He had served his time as a stoker in submarines in the Royal Navy and his colourful reminiscences passed many a long term of duty. Reg owned a motor cycle with a box-type sidecar which normally carried his tools. One evening, while we were on duty at the far end of Trentham Park, Kenneth Bailey (of password fame) asked Reg for a lift but after a fast cross-country ride, was visibly shaken and never asked again. Reg had a brother-in-law named Fred, who was a plasterer by trade but a countryman at heart. During a spell of duty in a field, we were surrounded by curious cattle. To reassure an anxious townsman, Fred grasped the nearest cow by the nose with one hand and an udder with the other, and then sprayed the townsman with milk to show that cows were harmless.

Our training was quite vigorous and included unarmed combat, rifle shooting, and the use of hand-grenades – later, we had Browning machine guns sent over from Canada. My car at the time was a Talbot 65 Saloon which was big enough to carry a machine gun section consisting of gun, tripod and six men. Consternation was caused by a demonstration for the benefit of senior officers seated on the stage in the parish hall, when the gun was smartly mounted on its tripod pointing straight at them and loaded with 250 rounds of live ammunition. We had two full nights' duty a week manning road blocks or observation posts and there were evening and Sunday morning training parades. These proved quite popular with married men as it gave them an alibi to visit the local before returning home. With the introduction of fire-watching I spent two nights a week at the factory as well, with no concession to working hours.

My friendship with Margaret had been shared, very amicably, on a sort of rota basis with Ian and in 1942, she gently told me that the pendulum of attachment had swung in his favour, and we parted good friends. Then I met Joan. Joan had more expensive tastes than Margaret but was very good company. After a platonic relationship lasting two years we had a brief meeting in London and a passionate embrace at the end of which I found myself engaged to be married. I bought her an exotic ring with baguette diamonds. We saw little more of each other and, like a fast-growing flower, our engagement wilted. I asked her to keep the ring as a memento of the affair which, I am glad to say, she did.

To my great relief, in the Spring of 1943 I was called up for military service. I set off for primary training to the Copthorne Barracks in Shrewsbury where leisure activities outweighed the rigours of army life. A good library, rowing on the river in the evenings, and unit dances enlivened by

Left, the fashionable Margaret wearing a necklace made of ping pong balls decorated with nail varnish, with Jean and her sister, Mary, Trentham Swimming Pool, 1941.

the friendship of a charming girl called Valerie Liddell, a dancer with the Ballet Rambert, who lived nearby. By this time the assessment of recruits had been introduced in order to direct them to the units for which they were best qualified. With my knowledge of languages, I was recommended to volunteer for the Intelligence Corps. This meant a trip to London for the interview. After spending the night in an army hostel, it gave me great pleasure and was a boost to my morale to have breakfast in the Piccadilly Hotel dressed in a private's uniform. At my interview I was questioned in great detail, even about my sporting activities of which I was pleased to list nine: golf, hockey, tennis, squash, badminton, table tennis, skating, skiing and swimming. Great assets for intelligence work! I was duly accepted.

From Shrewsbury I was sent to a holding depot in Bradford, Yorkshire, to await posting to my next unit. Here I was lucky – the general occupation was fatigues, i.e. labouring activities. I was detailed to report as a runner which involved spending the day in an office with a couple of smart A.T.S. girls, and taking messages to various parts of the unit when required. One fine Sunday afternoon, with three of my fellow recruits for the Intelligence Corps, I walked across the moor to Ilkley, intending to return by bus. As we made the precipitous descent from the moor, we saw the ominous sight of a long queue for a relatively small vehicle. As feared, it proved to be the last bus back to Bradford and there was no hope even of standing room. The thought of just climbing back up to the moor, let alone the twelve mile walk, was horrific. My mind ticked over. Douglas Waddilove, a very good friend of mine at Rugby, had lived in Ilkley. No harm in trying. His father answered the phone. I explained the situation and asked if he could give me the number of a local taxi firm. 'Come on up to the house,' he said and gave me directions. 'I have to go to Bradford tonight or tomorrow morning, so I may as well go now.' Four bedraggled, private soldiers, trudged up the hill to a massive stone-built mansion overlooking the town. The sun was still burning hot. We turned into a broad drive leading up

Home on leave, 1943. Father, myself and little John sitting under the pergola at Glendair.

to the house and were greeted by a tall figure in colonel's uniform. We saluted as smartly as we could. 'Come and sit down lads,' he said, and we walked up the drive to some garden seats. His slender wife appeared wearing an ice-blue trouser suit; nine years earlier she had shocked her son by attending a Rugby School Speech Day in a Paris outfit, open sandals and painted toe nails. 'Get the boys a jug of beer,' said her husband, and she returned in no time with a large foaming jug and four tankards. Bliss!

Refreshed and well-entertained, it was time to move on. Colonel Waddilove no longer had the replica of Queen Mary's massive Daimler in which he used to come to Rugby, but a car more suited to petrol rationing. He drove us back to our unit where the entrance was permanently guarded by R.P. (Regimental Police). 'May as well do it in style,' he said, 'I'll get out first.' The two R.Ps snapped to attention with quivering salutes. Four private soldiers scrambled out of the car, thanked the Colonel profusely, saluted and returned to barracks.

To prepare us for action we were sent to Richmond, Yorkshire, for three months' infantry training. Fine summer weather made this a pleasant experience. Interviewed by my Commanding Officer, I was asked what I thought of the army. 'So far, sir,' I replied, 'I have found it a complete rest cure.' In response to his surprise, I explained that I enjoyed exercise, that it was the first time in over two years that I had more than three full nights' sleep a week, and I now enjoyed a mid-morning tea break which I had never previously experienced. My fitness was shown when I ran two miles in eleven minutes, wearing army boots, and came in second out of 800 men.

Having completed the training period, we went once more to a holding depot to await posting where we were sent out to pick cabbages. I promptly asked for an interview with my C.O. and told him that if this was the best work available, I should be better employed at my father's factory producing exports. Result – seven days leave. I spent this at the Moorcroft factory and, while there, experienced a problem with Customs and Excise. American servicemen had found the factory and were spending substantial sums on gifts to send home to their families. The parcels were to be mailed through the U.S. army. The Customs officer said that this was insufficient proof of export. Sensing that my father was about to erupt, I quietly offered a solution. 'Type instructions on a letter heading with a statement that H.M. Customs and Excise will not accept the word of a US army officer. Mr Brown, the Customs officer, can then sign over H.M. Customs rubber stamp.' The question was permanently shelved.

At last training began in earnest. We were based at Wentworth Woodhouse near Rotherham – the home of Earl Fitzwilliam, and said to be the largest house in England – our accommodation was in the stables, magnificent buildings in their own right. Our training included learning to ride a motor cycle and to improve control, we rode up and down seemingly vertical slag heaps at the local colliery and covered miles of the Yorkshire Moors where we used to stop at a tiny cafe in Penistone for tea and marmalade sandwiches.

September 1944, our motor cycling class takes a rest on the Yorkshire Moors. I am in the centre sitting on the wall.

We were brought down to earth when we were given three weeks, under Guards' discipline, in which to learn the complete structure of the British Army – from General Officer Commanding down to the smallest unit of a section led by a corporal, plus all ancillary troops at Army level, Corps level and Divisional level, together with the rank of officers in command. There were some quite extraordinary ranks but the one that appealed to me most was the D.A.Q.M.G., Deputy Assistant Quartermaster General. At the end of the course we had a written examination with a pass mark of 90%. We had to work.

From Wentworth we went to Matlock for intensive lectures on intelligence – the collection, collation and correlation of information – and were fully briefed on the paramilitary organisations of France, Belgium and Holland. Our lectures were on the fourth floor of one hotel and our accommodation was on the fifth floor of another. In the interest of power economy there were no lifts, so we were not short of exercise. When this training was complete I acquired the rank of sergeant, supplemented by an officer's identity card with an endorsement giving me almost unlimited freedom of movement.

In the New Year of 1944 I was posted to No.11 Field Security Section, H.Q. 51st Welsh Division near Maidstone. A section consisted of the Commanding Officer (Captain) and his batman driver, and twelve men. Our C.O., Captain Robert Hyde Urquart, height 6ft 2ins, auburn hair (his own description), wore a scarlet Cameron Highlander's kilt which matched his personality. He was said to have a mistress on either side of Maidstone and his loyal batman driver ferried him from one to the other. Having very little knowledge of languages he decided to test ours, but was humiliated by a Welshman who changed from German into Welsh without the Captain noticing the difference.

We spent a relatively uneventful five months in preparation for the invasion of Europe. Apart from riding for miles on our motor cycles on various manoeuvres, we had an interesting break in London where we attended a course of lectures on booby traps and sabotage. Lord Rothschild, an expert in this field, delivered these talks with great lucidity, while chain-smoking Abdullah Egyptian cigarettes.

Action Across the Channel

I found time to buy a camembert cheese and drink a glass of calvados...

D-Day arrived. It was time to move on which was no bad thing as V1 flying bombs were coming over with considerable regularity. No one knew quite what they were, but a local inhabitant claimed that an old lady of his acquaintance had been hit right on the head with one! On a scorching hot Sunday we loaded our bikes on to open three-ton trucks, and scrambled on top. Cheered by crowds, we drove in a long convoy through the east end of London, until we reached Tilbury Docks. There, we boarded a Liberty ship, a vessel mass-produced in America with a welded, rather than riveted, hull. Eventually we set sail and the channel was crowded with processions of ships as far as the eye could see.

As we approached the French coast we amused ourselves by catching jelly fish in a bucket lowered over the side on a rope. It was now D+15 (fifteen days after D-Day) so quite comfortable. The way ashore was unconventional. The truck with our bikes had been transferred to an L.C.V. (landing craft for vehicles) which was heaving up and down in the swell. We went over the side of the ship on a scrambling net and on the command 'drop', we let go and were aboard the L.C.V. Safely ashore we made our headquarters in a farmhouse a few miles from Arromanches with a beautiful orchard and a convenient hayloft for sleeping quarters. The farm had a huge vat of home-brewed cider which we consumed with respect after a warning concerning its strength. The farmer told us that they used the cider as a weapon against their German guards during the occupation. A litre at lunchtime put the guards to sleep and freed the French from forced labour in the afternoon.

The Normandy bridgehead was now about fourteen miles long by four miles wide, so there was room in which to move about. I made a reconnaissance trip to Bayeux where I found time to look round the cathedral, buy a camembert cheese and drink a glass of calvados in a bar. Captain Urquart took me on a nocturnal recce in the jeep. I remember a beautiful church tower illuminated against the night sky by the flashes of our artillery in action. It was reassuring to feel that if we were near our guns, the enemy was some way off. Eventually we moved on but were halted in a farmyard as things were happening ahead. The weather broke and the heavens opened. The dusty earth changed to liquid mud and as I sat astride my stationary bike, it slipped in the mud and rolled over. Apart from a slight twinge in my ankle there seemed to be no problem. At 5.00am, I extracted my razor from my kit and shaved using water from a puddle. Maybe the fact that I was the only freshly shaven member of the section was the reason why I was chosen to go on a solo recce to find a unit which eluded me completely as the terrrain differed entirely from my map, owing to the construction of a new air strip and the annihilation of some of the narrow lanes by tanks.

At the end of a long day we made our headquarters at a fortified farmhouse with a huge courtyard designed to protect the livestock from the wars of past centuries. When I eventually took my boots off, my ankle was green, yellow and swollen. The next morning the C.O. took me in the jeep to base hospital for a check-up. I was supplied with a cup of tea and a cigarette by an attractive girl wearing a white coat on which a gold-printed label stated she was a 'Physiotherapist'. I sat on a packing case for an X-ray and when my ankle was declared broken, was put on to a stretcher in a large tent alongside rows of other stretcher cases. The *Last Post* sounded. 'It's okay chaps,' said the orderly, 'only a couple of dozen out of the last two thousand.' Hours passed. The stretchers were then loaded on to troop carriers, then off-loaded on to a launch which was hauled up the side of the hospital ship moored offshore. The stretchers were stacked in racks on board.

We crossed to Southampton where we were taken to a large hospital equipped to deal with the emergencies. Less urgent cases like myself and a chap in the artillery who had had a twenty-five pound shell dropped on his foot, were fully documented, issued with basic kit and put on a train which seemed to go on forever, until we finally arrived at Dundee. We were met at the station by members of the Dundee Bowling Club, stalwart volunteers who loaded the stretchers on to an ambulance for the journey to the local hospital. Here there was a lovely little nurse whom I nicknamed 'Squirrel' because she was very small and scuttled everywhere. My ankle steadily improved and I became a 'walking casualty' wearing 'hospital blues' which consisted of a bright blue jacket instead of a khaki tunic. I then moved on for further convalescence at the home of Lord Kinnaird, a beautiful place halfway between Dundee and Perth.

To qualify for return to active service a further four weeks' convalescence (now in army uniform rather than blue jackets), was scheduled at Glencorse outside Edinburgh. On arrival I told the M.O. (Medical Officer) that as my unit was motorised, and I was walking well, I felt ready to return to action. Wearing new boots, I was duly sent on a six-mile route march, which I survived and was told, as a result, that my convalescence would be reduced from four to three weeks. I was then programmed for remedial exercises. The time at Glencorse passed quickly as the weather was brilliant and a 'Liberty' truck provided transport into Edinburgh every evening. I had become friendly with the victim of the twenty-five pound shell as we shared the common experience of unheroic evacuation from the war zone. We ate leisurely meals at McVities in Princes Street and together explored the sights from Edinburgh Castle to the top of Arthur's Seat.

Intelligence Work in Europe

I found interrogation a fascinating challenge but a considerable responsibility...

At last I returned to Wentworth where I joined No.318 section. I immediately felt at ease with my new companions and we became regular customers at the Rockingham Arms named after the Marquises of Rockingham and the Earls Fitzwilliam who had lived in Wentworth since the thirteenth century. The passage of time was also helped by Joyce, who taught me the art of the sensual embrace – we spent four blissful hours watching Ernest Hemingway's *For Whom The Bell Tolls* at the local cinema. In preparation for our departure I was allocated my own 15 cwt truck which was far more civilised than a motor bike. We set off in an independent convoy headed by our C.O., Captain Milbank Watson, in an American jeep with two 15 cwt trucks and six motorcycles. We then made a relatively easy journey from Rotherham to Brussels via Normandy, where the Mulberry harbour was now fully operative.

We arrived early in December 1944, and received a series of lectures briefing us on our duties on entry into Germany. We were to round up the particularly undesirable members of the Nazi Party, identify them through interrogation, and then send them on for imprisonment or further interrogation at a higher level. In order to achieve this we had to learn about the general structure of the party and who we were looking for. Its correct title was the N.S.D.A.P., the *Nazional Sozialisticher Deutsche Arbeiter Partei*. As membership had been compulsory since 1937, we were looking for founder members and those holding high rank in its various subdivisions, with the exception of the S.S. and S.D. who were automatically on the wanted list. The significance of the S.S. is well-known, but the S.D. or *Sicherheitsdienst* (Security Service) had its headquarters in Berlin at the *Reichssicherheitshauptamt* which had separate offices for *Abwehr* (espionage), S.D. and Gestapo (*Geheimestaatspolizei* – Secret State Police). The S.D. was responsible for watching over the behaviour of the population through a network of *Leiters* (leaders), *Blockleiter* (those covering a few streets), *Zellenleiter*, *Ortsgruppenleiter*, *Kreisleiter* and *Gauleiter*, each responsible for a wide area of political control. Anyone deemed to transgress in speech or action would be dealt with by the Gestapo.

There was, however, more to Brussels than lectures. The city was full of life; we were entertained by local inhabitants and frequented the dance halls and cafes, the best of which were in the Rue Neuve. I acquired a pleasant girlfriend called Georgette who invited me to join a Christmas Eve party with some friends, with a request to be there at 4.00pm in order to get a good table. We talked, danced and drank a little. As midnight approached, I thought the festivities would end. No sign. At 1.00am I said, 'I really must be going.' 'Okay, you go when you want, we are staying till the trams start at 5.00.' I went! On Christmas Day, after an excellent lunch, I went to a symphony concert in the Galerie des Beaux Arts with the Halle Orchestra conducted by Sir John Barbirolli.

After leaving Brussels I had a postcard from Georgette which began, 'My father has Summer very ill.' The penny dropped – *Mon pére a été tres malade'* – laborious translation from a dictionary. She knew no English, and her charm was greater than her brain. As the New Year approached it was reported that with the help of captured jeeps and uniforms, there had been German infiltration of the American lines. We were sent down to the Ardennes together with the Highland Light Infantry to sort them out. On 1st January we arrived in Huy sur Meuse where the vital bridge over the river was said to have been saved from destruction by the local barber defusing the explosives. It was bitterly cold with impacted snow on the roads.

Headquarters were set up in the Rue d'Italie, a very steep hill sometimes used by the locals for tobogganing. We joined in the fun, and made ourselves popular by using the jeep to tow sledges to the top. We occupied Number 15 Rue d'Italie, and the Dodements lived at Number 12 where we spent many evenings with Mme. Dodement and her two daughters, Marie-Therese and Nicole, improving our French. Marie-Therese gave me an embroidered ram's head emblem which she wore for identification when working with the resistance. To make more room at Number 15, Sergeant Braithwaite and I moved out. My diary entry reads:

> '9th January 1945. Arrival at new billet. Central heating. Featherbed, marble windowsills. Private bathroom.'

This was the home of M. and Mme. Meerschaut and their daughter, Vivianne. M. Meerschaut was, amongst other things, a wine and spirit merchant; he had an enormous desk in his office downstairs which incorporated a drink cupboard containing some excellent brandy.

Our operational duty in Huy was focused mainly on cars and pedestrians crossing the bridge over the Meuse. One man I checked had the name J. Goebels – he had to be genuine! It gave me great pleasure to stop a large American Staff Car. The door opened showing three Generals on the back seat. The Four Star General turned to the Three Star who turned to the Two Star to supply identification. The Four Star was General Bradley. 'What is this about Sergeant?' he asked. 'British Intelligence Sir, checking movement control in the American Zone.' They drove on. When General Montgomery drove past the next day, I decided that it was diplomatic not to interfere.

The weather remained extremely cold. The C.O. sent me on a trip to Brussels in the jeep with Sergeant Norman Fellowes as a travelling companion. When driving through open country with an unfenced railway line alongside the road, we suddenly came to a sheet of ice. The jeep spun round, cartwheeled over the railway line, and finished upside down in a field. I jumped out in mid-air but Norman, who was a good linguist but not very agile, remained trapped underneath. Some farmworkers came to help and we gently rolled the jeep over and released Norman who was semi-conscious, but not seriously injured. An ambulance came in sight. I flagged it down and he was taken on board. Although damaged, the jeep was mostly in one piece. I picked up the windscreen and put it on the back seat, engaged four-wheel drive, and drove over the railway line back on to the road. I spotted a U.S. Army police sergeant and reported the accident. He made a few notes on his notepad, tore off a copy and gave it to me. 'Okay Bud – good luck.' After my C.O. recovered from his spontaneous outburst, 'My God! you've ruined my jeep,' it was put into the U.S. Army workshop from which it returned two days later with a new roof, new windscreen, new steering wheel and three new wheels.

At the end of February we bade farewell to our friends in Huy sur Meuse and headed for Holland with a brief stay in Oisterwijk before going on to Neimegen. Here we had a ground floor apartment with civilian neighbours upstairs. They were very helpful and delighted to have our white bread in exchange for their coarse wholemeal variety which we enjoyed. We engaged a competent local lad as our cook and he was thrilled with the ingredients available to him. One of his special dishes was lamb marinaded in milk and vinegar for twenty-four hours, diced, then fried in butter – quite different. In Neimegen we had our first subject for interrogation, a local collaborator. We compiled a dossier which ensured him a very uncomfortable future, if any future at all. We found what had been the office of the S.D. They had removed or destroyed as much as possible before their retreat but, amongst the few remaining papers, was a personal letter which ended, '*Dein liebe Gertrud. Heil Hitler.*'

The Rhine had now been crossed and it was time for us to follow. We were given a map reference, which led to an altercation between the C.O. and the Sergeant Major. After crossing the Remagen bridge three times within an hour, the argument remained unsettled and we split into two parties. I stayed with the C.O. After a sortie into the American spearhead, a course which was obviously wrong, we headed north with fresh directions, passing scores of gliders crash-landed for the original assault across the river and reached our correct destination in the Canadian zone. The Sergeant Major's party had, for some reason, turned south towards Dusseldorf and were arrested. However, once their identity had been established they were put on course and eventually caught up with us.

We established headquarters at Lingen and acquired our first German car, a rickety version of a Citroen Deux Chevaux. We were confronted by a formidable lady called Frau Tebbenhof who arrived with her daughter, complaining bitterly about her treatment by the Americans. After interrogation I was detailed to take them home using the car. They directed me along a cross-country track marked 'Not Cleared For Mines' but they obviously knew better. I deposited them at their country mansion and had great satisfaction some weeks later to find a male Tebbenhof listed in the Bremen S.S. files. Before entering Germany we had been warned of a possible resistance movement known as 'Werewolves'. One evening as we returned from a recce, two figures leaped out of the shadows. We did not stop to enquire about their motives. I drove my 15 cwt truck straight at them, and they ran.

The centre of Bremen, May 1945. My first impression of the bombing captured by my pocket camera.

Our next stop was Wesenstedt, ten miles south of Bremen, where once more we found a magnificent farmhouse, an orchard and hot sunshine. The peace was only disturbed by the crunch of 10,000 pound bombs being dropped on Bremen, prior to the final assault. On Thursday 26th April, we moved up to the outskirts of Bremen and I quote from my diary:

> 'After driving through an almost impenetrable cloud of dust we are told not to go into certain adjoining streets as Gerry is still there. We start a picnic on the grass verge

and sit in the sun. The infantry comes up to clear the streets. We recce one or two streets and pick up some wine. We drink the wine. News comes up that the next few blocks have been cleared – we move in to find a billet. We finally settle this by acquiring some flats further down the road. Shrapnel starts falling – no-one takes any notice except an American. (Two days later) people are allowed out one hour each morning and afternoon, women only. Our domestic staff is installed. The beautiful daughter turns up uninvited but welcome.'

Bremen, 1945. Enjoying a roadside picnic while waiting for the infantry to clear the next set of blocks.

On Friday 27th, our first working day in Bremen, enquiries led to the discovery of the bodies of a man and wife in their drawing room. I was sent to investigate as my colleague who had found them had left too quickly, a pale shade of green. In armchairs on either side of a bay window were man, wife and blood. The man was wearing the uniform of an *Oberführer* in the S.A. (*Sturmabteilung* – the equivalent of a politically impregnated Territorial Army, but without the muscle of the S.S.). Fearing a fate based on Nazi standards he had shot his wife in the head, and then himself. As evidence of my visit I cut the badge of rank from his uniform and I still have it in my collection of memorabilia.

The North German Lloyd Shipping Line was known to have been used worldwide for German espionage as their offices in every port made perfect cover. Their Bremen office had escaped the bombing but had been stripped of all its records. My only find was a few telephone numbers written on a scrap of paper. When the very common name, Karl Schmidt, came to our attention a few days later, I compared my numbers with a telephone directory. To my great satisfaction one of them matched and I obtained his address. Herr Schmidt was of no great importance but he was much impressed by our efficiency.

My next task was at the Polizei Praesidium to interrogate every member of the Bremen police force. This was helped by a *fragebogen* or questionnaire on which to enter the details. All went well until I was confronted by a somewhat shrivelled character who seemed unable to understand me, nor I him. In desperation I wrote in block letters '*Sprechen sie Deutsch*'. It turned out that he was deaf and had a hair-lip, but was employed as the police tailor. A less arduous task was the investigation with my C.O. of Bremen Post Office. The spacious interior was in total chaos with postage stamps and bank notes scattered everywhere. I gathered several sheets of postage stamps and we both filled our pockets with bank notes as a souvenir of the occasion. The following day, much to our surprise, we found that they were valid and decided that they were legitimate spoils of war. I used my share to buy drink for our unit for the rest of my time in Germany. A wine merchant in Bremen was very pleased, saying that we were far better than the German army who just took wine without paying for it.

V.E. Day arrived and called for a celebration. Somehow, the C.O. had become acquainted with a Greek Cypriot, and a Spanish pianist called Juan Llossas, two omniscient characters well-fitted to survive. They organised a party with at least six nationalities among the guests, including German. Here I met Elsa and Lotti. Elsa became attached to my friend, Doug Huckle, and I became friendly with Lotti. We visited their flat most evenings which provided a pleasant interlude, beneficial, amongst other things, to our knowledge of German. Fraternization was strictly prohibited, but this was 'in the course of duty'. Following the end of hostilities, the civilian population appeared as if from nowhere and, with amazing efficiency, cleared up what remained of the city. The higher-ranking members of the Nazi party had fled, so our work was largely confined to searching buildings. These included an enormous air-raid shelter, like a honeycomb of concrete, in which a twenty-nine year old S.S. officer, securely underground, had held out while the city was being destroyed by bombing.

Eventually, we moved north through Schleswig Holstein and on the 22nd of May arrived in Flensburg. I went ahead with my C.O. to take take over our billet from the previous occupants. They were having a farewell party at the centre of which was a large bowl of punch. I asked for a sample of the strongest alcohol in the mix. I was told it was arrack, a potent concoction of locally distilled alcohol. I duly informed my C.O. and instead, fetched a bottle of whisky from my room. We were the only two to eat breakfast the next morning.

Flensburg was a small, picturesque town on the Danish frontier at the head of a fjord separating the two countries. It had a substantial harbour and a hinterland of beautiful countryside where storks could be seen nesting in the roofs of farm buildings. Our H.Q was Woest's Hotel, ideal for our requirements as it had a substantial lounge bar, about fifteen bedrooms, office accommodation and a good kitchen. We installed an excellent cook and a general housemaid, enlisted from the local population. One of the bedrooms became the interrogation room where I spent a lot of my time. I adjusted my dress to suit the environment,

Woest's Hotel, our H.Q. in Flensburg, May 1945.

I am in the driving seat of our military Volkswagen adapted from 'the people's car', 1945.

wearing an American shirt, an officer's tie and no badges of rank; a Walther automatic, which held six 9mm rounds in the butt, fitted snugly into my hip pocket. With the final surrender of the O.K.W. (*Oberkommando der Wehrmacht* – Army High Command), Admiral Doenitz was 'invited out to breakfast' which he was alleged to have attended wearing seven pairs of underpants, for reasons best known to himself. The ceremony did not directly concern us, but is worth recording.

Not far from Flensburg was Glucksburg Castle, a fairytale building with pink capped turrets at each corner, and surrounded by a large lake. A group of important people, including relations of the English royal family, had taken refuge there in order to get as far away as possible from bombing and military action. We were called upon to check their identity while the castle was searched for any weapons or hostile equipment. It was not known what kind of reception we would receive, so no risks were taken. A party was made up, led by armoured jeeps, followed by a small section of infantry, the press, then ourselves, with a field gun covering the castle from the far side of the lake in case of emergency. We literally thundered across the drawbridge in the style of yesteryear. There was no resistance and our reception was quite civilised.

While the premises were being searched, the occupants of the castle were evacuated into the courtyard awaiting interrogation, then put back inside awaiting dispersal as required. I spent the day in the courtyard and had the satisfaction of interrogating among many others, Prince Willie, a weak and unimposing character who was a relation of the royal family, and Albert Speer, the Nazi party's official architect who, by contrast, was tall, saturnine and emanated dignity in defeat. At the end of the day the driver of a German army Volkswagen came to me in search of his passenger, a senior Staff Officer. As I had returned the officer awaiting internment to the castle, I told the man to give me the keys and go on his way. The Volkswagen was a glorified tin box on wheels with a wonderful performance. I drove it for miles. Before the war, its production had been financed by universal subscription for 'The People's Car – Volkswagen'. Unfortunately for the people, the dream car became a military vehicle.

I spent most of my time in the interrogation room at Woest's Hotel but made occasional trips outside, which had their lighter moments. When visiting a displaced person's camp, there were some rather doubtful characters wandering about and I fired my automatic for the only time in public. I took a pot shot at a bottle lying on the grass and rather surprisingly hit it, which produced the required respect from the people in the vicinity. A rewarding incident was the acquisition of a very fine car by the simple expedient of arresting its occupants. The passengers in the car (a large Auto Union Convertible),

Glucksburg Castle, a refuge for V.I.Ps, 1945.

were senior officers of the *Reichsarbeitsdienst* (the Labour Corps) whose rank I recognised by their uniform. Despite possession of a pass issued by 2nd Army H.Q. they were 'arrestable material'. So we committed them to gaol and kept the car. My C.O. took an immediate fancy to it but allowed me to drive it occasionally.

I found interrogation a fascinating challenge but a considerable responsibility. One had the power to make or break each subject and, as many of them were quite innocent, it was as important to impress upon them the difference between British and German methods, as it was to intimidate and incarcerate the guilty. From the innocent and guilty alike we built up a complete record of information which was recorded on a card index. Flensburg was the last staging post on the route of Swedish Red Cross convoys before the Danish frontier, and these were used by a number of Nazis in their attempts to escape from the country – attempts which we had much pleasure in frustrating. As a result of arresting a Senior S.S. officer, I acquired a Totenkopf ring. This had the death's head and other insignia of the S.S. on the outside and, on the inside, the signature of Heinrich Himmler plus the name of the wearer. I wore it conspicuously for the benefit of my 'clients'. An acquisition which I did not wear, was the Gestapo identity disc, No.253. I received the wearer at gunpoint as he was delivered to our front door at midnight. There was no problem in identification so we committed him forthwith to the local gaol. We only once had to use crude methods of interrogation and this was in the case of a member of the S.D. whose documents made him out to be his own illegitimate half-brother. We said afterwards that he was the only Nazi we had met who called himself a bastard. His papers had been issued in Essen after the destruction of the records office by allied bombing, and we were warned that such papers were almost invariably false as the office was no longer functioning. We stripped him naked, removed his cyanide pill (kept for suicide in an emergency) and persuaded him to talk.

I am seen here wearing the Totenkopf ring.

Our information network picked up a few females but we found it expedient, after applying a little pressure which bordered on blackmail, to give them their freedom. One exception was Frau Schreibmeyer who had been Himmler's personal telephonist. She had to be passed on for detailed interrogation but before doing so, I took her photograph for my records. Fräulein Anna Schmidt had arrived on one of the Swedish Red Cross Convoys and was able to give me some useful information. She had worked for the equivalent of the Ministry of Supply in Berlin and expressed her amazement that the British and Americans had stopped their advance when Germany surrendered, instead of driving the Russians back to their original frontiers. We let her settle into her own flat on the condition that she did not leave Flensburg but she rashly decided to do so and set off by train. I went in pursuit in the Auto Union and caught up with her at a station about fifteen miles down the line. As I escorted her from the train to the car, I told her that she would be able to listen to the Hamburg Symphony Orchestra on the car radio as we drove back to Flensburg. She was most ungrateful but too well-bred to spit.

My photograph of Frau Schreibmeyer, Himmler's personal telephonist, Flensburg, 1945.

The American weakness for a pretty face provided us with an interesting arrest. An attractive young woman who had worked as a clerk in the S.D. succeeded in finding employment in a U.S. Army office for three weeks, before travelling north to Flensburg. With her arrival in the British Zone she was due for a shock. After a long journey she had retired to bed and was awakened the next morning when we knocked on her front door. Other than supplying us with one name, which we passed on to our colleagues in Hamburg, she was of no great importance but we were smugly satisfied with the impression we had made by picking her up within twelve hours of arriving in the British Zone after three weeks of paid employment with the U.S. Army.

Flensburg Harbour contained a lot of shipping and a Naval M.L. (a 70-foot boat) was moored alongside the main waterfront. The Lieutenant in command invited me and a colleague to look around his ship and the tour ended with an invitation to have a drink. We went down below where he opened a hatch and pulled out a large stoneware container of naval rum and poured about an inch of the fiery liquid into tin mugs. Two days later, he turned up at our office demanding the instant arrest of a dejected German youth. 'Dumb insolence,' he said, 'standing staring at my ship.' We had no option but to question the lad who, it transpired, had escaped from a prisoner-of-war camp and so had to be sent back.

To help us in our liaison with Denmark, an ubiquitous character called Fred was attached to our unit. Fred was a Dane who had been trained to make parachute drops with money and supplies for the resistance movement. He had eventually escaped from Denmark via Sweden and thence in the bomb rack of a diplomatic *Mosquito* aircraft. Fred had his own car with Danish documents to use in Germany and British documents for use in Denmark and his black market deals, to and fro across the frontier, were discreetly ignored. I remember him saying, 'They trained me to behave like a crook in order to perform my duty. I now intend to reap the benefit.' Fred and I became good friends despite his insatiable appetite for my cigarettes. I checked this by keeping a foul-smelling German cigarette in my case, which I offered when I felt that he had smoked quite enough of my Players No.3.

The local policeman, a dashing character who rushed around Flensburg on his motor bike, became a regular visitor to our establishment. While having a drink together one evening, we had agreed on the total folly of the war. I then said that the British and Germans had much in common and we could well come back together in the future. His eyes lit up with Teutonic zeal. 'Then we should have the world at our feet,' he exclaimed, ready to start all over again. Flensburg, in the extreme north of Schleswig Holstein, had escaped a lot of the indoctrination of the Nazi party and we made some good friends among the local inhabitants. One of them asked me a very pertinent question. 'We are puzzled,' he said, 'by the result of the election in England. How is it that, having spent six years destroying a National Socialist government in Germany, the British have elected a Socialist government with a policy of nationalisation?' I explained that it was a case of similar words having a different meaning.

The local policeman in Flensburg on his motorbike.

As well as serious discussion we also enjoyed female company, notably Gertrud and her sister, Heidi. I was initiated into the ceremony of *bruderschafttrinken* which permitted the use of the familiar *du* instead of *sie*, a form of address known as *dusagen* which is the same as the French *tutoyer*. To perform the ceremony the man takes a glass of wine in his right hand and the girl takes one in her left. They then sit side by side with their arms around each other's necks and drink simultaneously out of each other's glass.

Gertrud, one of our local friends in Flensburg.

It was a hot summer and as we were now getting a few hours of leisure time, we found a sandy beach on the Baltic where we could drive by jeep down to the water's edge. At first our swimming was somewhat inhibited by the number of jelly fish, but we realised that they must be harmless when we saw the locals throwing them at each other – a diversion in which we did not participate!

Eventually I got ten days home leave, which meant a long railway journey with a night in a transit camp where we slept in a large reception area. In the morning a fellow traveller demanded, 'Who the hell are you?' I told him and asked why the question. 'Because you have been talking bloody German all night,' he replied.

Running the Company

I was now managing director, works manager, personnel manager and art director...

Autumn 1945 and a civilian once more. On Saturday the 19th September 1945, I received a telegram stating that my father had suffered a stroke and was dying. We had close contact with 2nd Army Headquarters, and my C.O. made immediate arrangements for compassionate leave and a flight to England, which I made in a freight aircraft. I reached London just in time to catch the last train north, arriving in Stoke at 1.00am. After a short sleep I was ready to take control of the factory on Monday the 1st of October. I did not return to Germany, as my leave was extended until formal demobilisation could be arranged.

Although my father was unable to speak, he could understand me. I was able to reassure him that all was well at the factory and that I had taken full control and it was obvious that this gave him great peace of mind. He died two weeks later on the 14th of October. After a service in Trentham Church, attended by a large congregation including most of the Moorcroft work people, my father was buried with my mother in the parish cemetery which adjoined the mausoleum erected for the Dukes of Sutherland.

My first priority was to establish with Liberty & Co., my official position in W. Moorcroft Limited, and my terms of employment by the company. This was facilitated by the fact that I was already a director of the company. Liberty's drew up a proposition, framed by their solicitor Harold Blackmore, who was related to Sir Arthur Liberty by marriage. He was renowned as a tough negotiator and held in awe by the staff of Liberty & Co. However, my experience of interrogating senior members of the Nazi party and the S.S. had provided me with a sound foundation for handling people and arrangements were soon agreed to my satisfaction. To consolidate the situation, I appointed an accountant and a solicitor, both of whom I knew personally. I then rejoined the British Pottery Manufacturer's Federation, where I was very well received despite the fact that my father had resigned his membership rather abruptly in the pre-war years because he disagreed with a requirement that members should pool their technical knowledge for the benefit of the newly formed Ceramic Research Association.

I was now managing director, works manager, personnel manager and art director of Moorcroft Pottery. I had no official training in art or ceramic technology – with hindsight, I feel that my father mistrusted the influence of the local school of art or technical college – but seven years' experience prior to my call up had given me a good working knowledge of general procedure. Although retaining theoretical autonomy, my father had come to rely more and more on my assistance. I drafted replies to nearly all his letters to keep him up-to-date with his correspondence. I cooperated with overseas buyers on the change of background colours, such as the *Leaf* design on blue instead of green, and the *Anemone* on green instead of blue. This did not always please my father who rebuked me once for suggesting that it might be better to supply a customer with the colour that he wanted rather than that which my father thought he ought to have. I spent a considerable time trying to coordinate the haphazard progress of our orders from the office to the packing table; on the technical side I monitored the firing of the bottle-ovens and the relatively simple procedures of mixing colours but, most importantly, I had, by close observation, acquired the sixth sense needed to control the *flambé* kiln.

The old time clock relegated to a place on the wall by the biscuit kiln.

Despite his declining health, my father had done a great job in keeping the factory going while I was away in the army. However, because of the stacks of pots everywhere, except for the actual production area of the factory, there was very little room to move. The centre of administration was the office, a sixteen-foot square room in the middle of the factory. One wall was lined with steel shelving containing files going back to the factory's opening in 1913; the next wall was taken up by a large filing cabinet and a cast iron radiator above which hung a mirror and a framed print illustrating Rodin's famous sculpture, *The Kiss*, which because of its nudity, caused the odd raised eyebrow from visitors. A square table and a typist's desk provided space for office work. My father's desk was piled high with papers and surrounded on the floor by bags of colour and other potters' materials. To complete the picture a pile of miscellaneous items obscured a large roll top desk, which had not been used for years. I had the bags of colour put into a cupboard outside the office and removed the debris from the desk so that we could, at least, invite a visitor to sit down. It was easy to criticise the congested state of the factory and many of its primitive methods of working but it was what the work people had been used to and the priority was to maintain production and make improvements as we went along.

Coal was rationed and some supplies were still delivered by horse and cart from the nearby Sneyd pit. We obtained our requirements without much difficulty but to make sure, we engaged the services of a local haulier who backed his truck up to the loading hopper at the colliery where it was filled without question. With the petrol shortage, horse-drawn transport continued to play its part and was used by British Rail for the daily collection of goods to be delivered to their depot in Hanley for dispatch to their ultimate destination. Charges for this service were collected by Mr Gimbert, an elderly railway clerk, who called every Friday afternoon. He had started his career on the old North Stafford Railway as an apprentice porter at Sandon Station near Stone, which served the needs of Lord Harrowby on whose estate the station was situated. To fulfil this duty he received full instructions concerning the correct behaviour when visiting Sandon Hall. I mention this to illustrate a way of life fast disappearing after two world wars.

The installation of electricity had already been considered and I put this in hand immediately. A large electric motor took the place of the old gas engine which drove our lathes and throwing wheels, and electric lighting illuminated parts of the factory which had depended solely on the light of day. It was some considerable time before I had the courage to put the time clock into use – it had been installed when the factory was built but had rested hidden by a cupboard ever since.

Manufacture for the home market was confined to undecorated tableware known as Utility Ware, and each manufacturer had to undertake to produce a monthly quota with the inevitable forms to be completed to substantiate this. Decorated export rejects could be sold under licence related to the value of export sales and were avidly sought after by the retail trade. After the lean years of trading in my earlier days it was quite exciting to have more orders than we could cope with, but it was necessary to be wary of tempting offers which might be accepted to the detriment of regular customers.

The Lightolier Company of New York with whom we had traded during the war, sent me a cable:

Packing ware for export. Woodwool was used because it was sterile – straw had to be disinfected and accompanied by a veterinary certificate, 1950s.

> 'Please ship at once 40,000 shillings worth of regular lines. We invite you urgently to come to New York at our expense to discuss arrangements to be your exclusive distributor to the U.S.A.'

40,000 shillings looked more impressive than £2,000. I cabled by return:

> 'Thank you for your order and invitation. Regret attention to the former, bars acceptance of the latter.'

About a month later, I received a phone call from a manufacturer in the Birmingham area who had accepted a similar invitation. He said that he had done a deal with them and that he had been assured by the head of the company, Mr Mo Blitzer, that I would tell him all about them. I had never heard of Mr Mo Blitzer – my dealings had all been with their buyer Max Daum. We maintained a good relationship with the Lightolier Company but, like everybody else, they had to be content with an allocation of our production.

About this time, our activity with the American market attracted the attention of the appraiser for U.S. Customs. The function of the appraiser was, for duty purposes, the assessment of the value of merchandise imported into the United States. Importers wanted the lowest figure, U.S. customs wanted the highest. If it could be proved that an item had been sold as a single unit at a price say, of £5, then offered to an importer at a discount of 25% for quantity, duty would be payable on the higher figure.

Throughout the war we had been supplying large quantities of lamp bases which were exclusive to the buyer at an agreed price. The appraiser wanted to prove that we would have charged more if we had sold them elsewhere, but we had not. After two hours of cross-examination in the office, I asked him sharply if he had brought his pyjamas with him as the last train to London left in half-an-hour. He abandoned play and caught his train. Two weeks later I had a phone call from him and he went over the details of our previous discussion. Once more, my experience of interrogation techniques served me very well and after a long conversation at his expense, he abandoned play for good.

As shipping lanes opened up, export orders poured in and as well as America and Canada we shipped to South Africa, North and Southern Rhodesia, Australia, New Zealand and the Caribbean. Amongst the more exotic places, we had a good account in Bogotá, the capital of Columbia. All export orders were packed in casks which were made to order in a number of sizes at the cooper's next door as, whenever possible, each shipment was packed in a single cask. Bogotá was an exception, as their orders had to be packed in casks small enough to fit one on each side of a mule in a mule train which made the 10,000 feet ascent from the coast. My customer told me that he could see the means of transport changing direct from mule train to aircraft before satisfactory highways were constructed.

In the home market, allocations of our export rejects were in great demand. With a few exceptions I gave preference to privately owned businesses rather than

Window display celebrating the Diamond Jubilee of Katz & Lourie of Johannesburg with my *Tiger Lily* vase displayed on the left, November 1955.

department stores and made some very good friends amongst customers both old and new, as they came to visit the factory. When the buyer from a chain of china shops notorious for harsh trading methods arrived, it gave me great pleasure to tell him that, based on their pre-war business with us, they might expect an allocation worth five shillings a quarter.

As I recalled earlier, artwork had been father's sole prerogative with the exception of the few pieces designed by me which, nevertheless, bore his signature. My first challenge was to meet the continual demand for repeat drawings or tracings, like a hand-drawn transfer, which were required for the application of the designs to the clay, prior to tube-lining the decoration. My father had always done this personally and I had been almost brainwashed with the idea that these drawings had to be done by a Moorcroft, or they would lose their identity. So I accepted a duty which I continued to perform for the next forty years. Many years later, I made reference to this when visited by Colin Mills (son of Herbert Mills), a very old customer from Hamilton, Ontario. He was astounded. 'Gee,' he exclaimed, 'you do all your own artwork! That must save you some money.' The designs in production were more than sufficient to meet the almost unlimited demand for decorated pieces, but I felt the necessity to prove both to myself and to others that I was not a slave to repetition. To achieve this, I selected a vase, seventeen inches high, which was the largest piece which we had in production at the time. Working from a watercolour sketch which I had done when at school, I created the *Tiger Lily* design. As the natural colouring was too delicate for such a large piece, I finished it off with reduction firing in my *flambé* kiln, producing rich reds and chartreuse green. Very few pieces were made but there is an outstanding example in the museum at the Moorcroft factory. The only record that I have of those that went abroad, is an illustration of a special display by Katz & Lourie of Johannesburg to celebrate their diamond jubilee.

My next design was derived from drawings of columbines which I had grown in my garden. In order to portray the delicacy of these flowers, I put them on a white background, shading to pale green at the base. As Moorcroft was still associated essentially with darker colours, only a few were made. My father had started the *Clematis* design on a few vase shapes. I recognised its potential and extended it across the whole range of our productions. Although my work, it was still my father's style and I was in need of inspiration. I had opened an

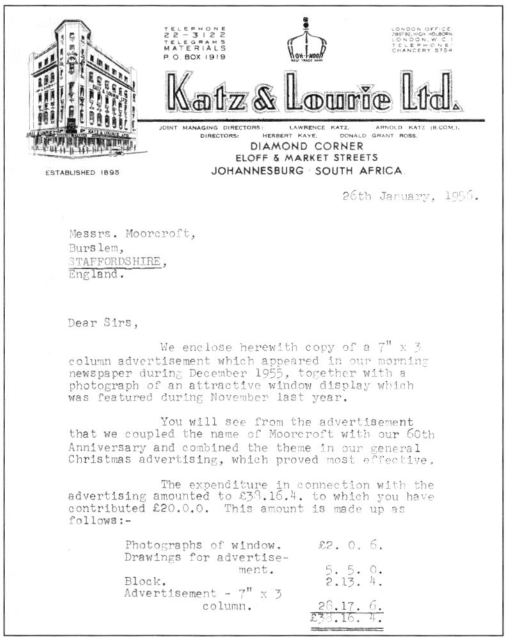

TELEPHONE 22-3122
TELEGRAMS MATERIALS
P.O. BOX 1919

LONDON OFFICE: 289/92, HIGH HOLBORN, LONDON, W.C.1
TELEPHONE: CHANCERY 5754

Katz & Lourie Ltd.

JOINT MANAGING DIRECTORS: LAWRENCE KATZ. ARNOLD KATZ (B.COM.).
DIRECTORS: HERBERT KAYE. DONALD GRANT ROSS.

DIAMOND CORNER
ELOFF & MARKET STREETS
JOHANNESBURG · SOUTH AFRICA.

ESTABLISHED 1895

26th January, 1956.

Messrs. Moorcroft,
Burslem,
STAFFORDSHIRE,
England.

Dear Sirs,

We enclose herewith copy of a 7" x 3 column advertisement which appeared in our morning newspaper during December 1955, together with a photograph of an attractive window display which was featured during November last year.

You will see from the advertisement that we coupled the name of Moorcroft with our 60th Anniversary and combined the theme in our general Christmas advertising, which proved most effective.

The expenditure in connection with the advertising amounted to £38.16.4. to which you have contributed £20.0.0. This amount is made up as follows:-

Photographs of window.	£2. 0. 6.
Drawings for advertisement.	5. 5. 0.
Block.	2.13. 4.
Advertisement - 7" x 3 column.	28.17. 6.
	£38.16. 4.

Letter from Katz & Lourie of Johannesburg, dated January 1955, acknowledging our contribution to the cost of their promotion.

account with the London Shop in Kingston, Jamaica, and when visiting the factory in 1949, their buyer said that he was sure that I would be interested in some of their exotic flowers. He sent me pressed examples of hibiscus and bougainvillaea together with watercolour drawings by a local artist. These provided me with just the material I required, and the hibiscus became as important to me as the pomegranate was to my father.

The pressed hibiscus sent to me from Jamaica in 1949.

Two of my first designs for production. Left, the *Columbine* drawing, 1947; right, an early *Hibiscus* drawing, 1949.

Powder Blue Tableware showing a toast rack of which each of the five bars was pressed out by hand then dipped in blue slip and joined to the base with liquid clay. Photographed by Odhams Press for *Ideal Home*, 1949.

In 1946, The Council of Industrial Design staged the 'Britain Can Make It Exhibition' and examples of *Moorcroft Blue Tableware* were included. The tableware played its part in keeping the Moorcroft name to the fore during a long period of antipathy to applied decoration in traditional style. It was selected again for the Festival of Britain in 1951 and it gave me great pleasure to enter the date of the design as 1913 in a catalogue mainly of 'Contemporary Designs' which were the buzz words of the day. Recognition came in the late 1950s when the tableware was featured in the permanent exhibition at the Design Centre in the Haymarket.

1945 – 1946 was an eventful period as it was the time when I took charge of my own destiny. Despite severe petrol rationing it was worth running a car. I sold my 1933 Lanchester Coupé with Albert Salmon's body (bought for 99 guineas in 1943), and acquired a 1934 SS Continental Saloon for £210. This was a formidable car with a spare wheel mounted in a metal case on either side of the bonnet. (The SS description was dropped after the war because of its sinister connections – the SS Jaguar became just Jaguar.)

Marriage to Molly

On 3rd November 1948, Jean was born...Sheila was born on the 19th of April 1951...

I kept fit with golf, squash, tennis and swimming. It was very pleasant to visit Trentham Swimming Pool on the way home from work and, before an evening swim, have afternoon tea served on the sun terrace above the changing rooms. Golf was my main recreation however, and in 1946, apart from winning my fifth solid silver trophy, I met Molly on the golf course. We were married on 7th December that year. Houses were at a premium and I bought a very small house on the Trentham Dairyfields Estate for £2200. This was owned by two spinsters who charged among the extras, ten shillings for a piece of linoleum on the lavatory floor. I asked my bank manager whether I should buy the house through the bank or a building society. He advised that if I bought through them, I would avoid a lot of formalities should I wish to acquire another property. I took him at his word and only four weeks later told him that I wanted to buy another property, Easedale, for £3,200, where I have now lived for over fifty years. The bank manager took it very well and hardly blinked when I also told him that my new car had at last arrived, a Rover 10 Saloon for £491. I may say that I only had a few hundred pounds in my account but banking was different in those days. I told my solicitor that I wanted to dispose of the first house at sufficient profit to cover incoming and outgoing costs. This was done with a small surplus of £20.

Trentham Swimming Pool with its glass-fronted cafe and sun terraces designed by Harold Goldstraw, of Wood, Goldstraw and Yorath, Architects, 1935.

For our honeymoon, Molly and I went to Totnes, spending our first night on the way at the Royal Hop Pole in Tewkesbury. Despite past encounters, I was still a novice in the act of love so Molly thoughtfully brought a clinical handbook with her which had its uses, but was soon set aside. In Totnes we stayed at the Chateau Bellevue (30s a day full-board), where we were greeted on arrival by two large glasses of port on our bedroom mantelpiece, a very welcome gesture on a December afternoon. The hotel dining room was beautifully equipped with starched white linen, and silver candlesticks. Wendy Hiller, the actress, was a fellow guest. As a souvenir of our honeymoon we bought a heavily carved corner chair which has been in the hall at Easedale ever since.

Easedale was built in 1900 as part of a development allowed by the Duke of Sutherland on his estate. At the end of a row of houses along the Longton Road it overlooked a dairy farm with a large orchard bordering one side of our garden. At the bottom of the garden, fields stretched as far as the eye could see and cows would come and stand at the hedge gazing with ruminant curiosity at our activities. Sadly the farm is now past history as it was sold in the 1960s and planning permission was granted for a substantial building estate.

Molly and I moved into Easedale on our mutual birthdays, 12th February 1947. It was a bitterly cold winter, reminiscent of 1940-41. We went skating on Alsager Mere as late as 15th March and, when the thaw finally came, the tarmac surface of the road through Trentham broke up like a ploughed field. Early in the year, I had a phone call from an inspector at Scotland Yard expressing the wish to speak to me the following day at Stoke-on-Trent Police Station. He was conducting an enquiry into events at Glucksburg Castle, Schleswig Holstein, in May 1945 – events which I have already described. It transpired that, after the castle had been evacuated and searched by British troops, £30,000 worth of jewellery and personal effects had been reported missing. I was relieved that, as I had spent that day in the courtyard interrogating witnesses, I was able to satisfy him concerning my movements. I heard no more from Scotland Yard or any report of their investigation which was not surprising, as two years had passed since the incident took place during the fluid state of affairs in post-war Germany.

Easter 1947 was spent at the Castle Hotel, Bangor, with our friends Roy Clark and his wife, Margaret. We travelled rather grandly in Roy's ancient Rolls Royce limousine which he called 'Clara'. In May 1947, the B.I.F. was again staged in London, now at Earls Court rather than Olympia as in the pre-war days. For the pottery industry it was purely a prestige exhibition as demand far exceeded supply. It was,therefore, decided that each participant should have an unmanned stand in a composite display to show that the industry was back in full production. Having completed the arrangement of my stand, I was asked by an official to be there if possible on the day Queen Mary visited the exhibition. The Queen arrived with, among others, Sir Stafford Cripps in attendance. I was introduced to her and she told me she was sorry to hear that her old friend had died and she wished me success for the future.

As a relief from the daily pressures of work, I continued the practice of lunching every day at the Grand Hotel in Hanley, where I had a permanently reserved table. This became the focal point for an interesting group of friends. Denys Kent (for whom I was best man at his wedding in 1941), was a research chemist working on electrical

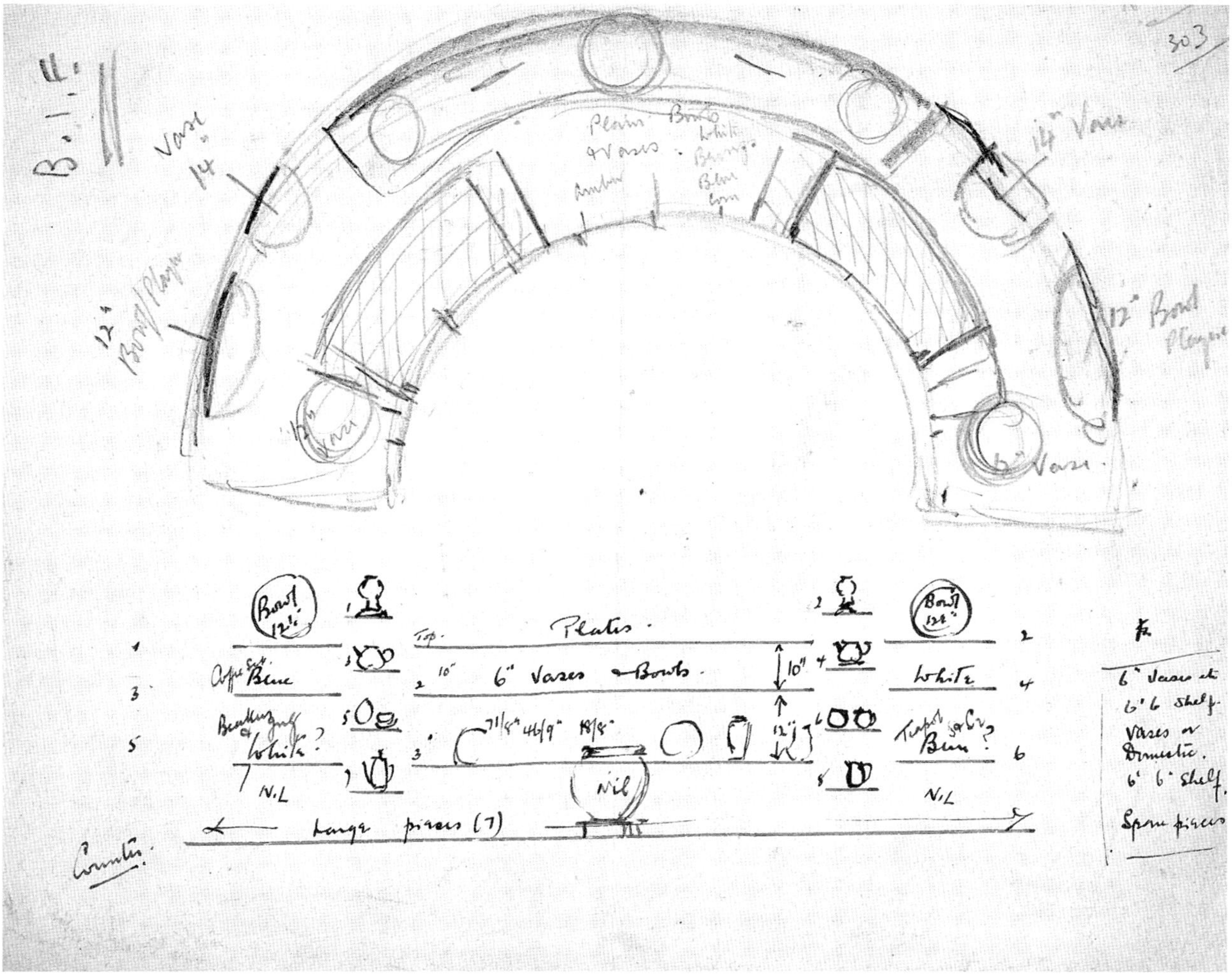

British Industries Fair 1947, my sketch plan for our display on a semi-circular fixture supplied to each exhibitor.

porcelain at Taylor Tunnicliffe's where his father, Sir John Kent, was managing director; John Moron, Denys' brother-in-law, solicitor and amateur historian, became a lifelong friend; Roy Clark, an accountant and part-time farmer; Alec Lovat, a scientist involved in the development of radar during the war, head of Acme Marls, manufacturing refractories for the ceramic industry; and Paul Bernard Roth, a poseur but a highly-respected orthopaedic surgeon at the North Stafford Royal Infirmary. To cope with the limitations of rationing, lunch menus included jugged hare, oxtail, pigeon pie, calves head and sweetbreads. The three-course lunch cost 3s 6d.

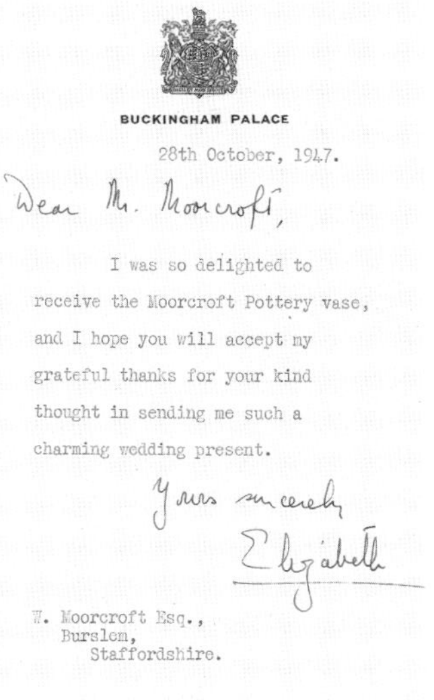
BUCKINGHAM PALACE

28th October, 1947.

Dear Mr. Moorcroft,

I was so delighted to receive the Moorcroft Pottery vase, and I hope you will accept my grateful thanks for your kind thought in sending me such a charming wedding present.

Yours sincerely

Elizabeth

W. Moorcroft Esq.,
Burslem,
Staffordshire.

Personal letter from Princess Elizabeth thanking me for her wedding present, a twelve-inch *Anemone flambé* vase, 1947.

In the summer we had a perfect holiday in Exmouth, stretching our petrol ration to the limit. We arrived in pouring rain but then the sun came out and shone for the entire two weeks. On a breezy afternoon I had my second and final experience of offshore fishing in a motor launch. (The first was off the South coast in 1931, with the same dire results.) I was violently sick, which would have been less embarrassing had I not been the only person visibly affected. To relieve my misery we were put ashore at a convenient village where we were able to catch a bus back to the hotel. I have not been fishing since.

The wedding of Princess Elizabeth and Prince Philip had been arranged to take place in November. As the holder of a Royal Warrant, my offer of a Moorcroft vase as a wedding present was accepted and acknowledged in a letter signed personally by the Princess. Formality was the order of the day and I duly received an invitation from the

Lord Chamberlain to attend Their Majesties' Afternoon Party at St. James's Palace on the 17th November for a private view of the wedding presents, which meant wearing morning dress and queuing. What impressed me most on entering the palace, was a large notice stating 'No Smoking – By Order The Ministry of Works'. The power behind the throne! It was a memorable occasion and the displayed gifts from worldwide potentates and diplomatic sources were breathtaking.

Early in 1948, exactly as planned, Molly became pregnant! On 3rd November, Jean was born. Her arrival was slow and painful and in the early evening I was told by the hospital not to phone again until 10.00pm. So, I went to the golf club to play bridge. At 10.00pm I was dummy, so I excused myself for a call of nature, phoned and learned that I had a daughter and that mother and child were both well. I returned to the card room without comment except for ordering a round of drinks. We finished the rubber and I went home. The following week, after the birth was announced in the local paper, I was greeted by one of my friends at the club. 'Congratulations! Weren't you playing bridge with us that evening, you crafty devil?' My response was that while I may have said nothing, I did buy a round of drinks!

In those days it was customary to have a nurse in the house for three or four weeks after childbirth. We had a stalwart character called Nurse Butt. One evening I had the symptoms of a cold. 'What you need,' she said, 'is a tablespoon of whisky at bedtime!' 'Thank you nurse,' I replied, 'I shall have more than a tablespoonful and shall have it in a cut glass.' To help with the laundering of nappies and baby clothes, Molly's father bought us a Bendix washing machine which was the very latest labour saving device.

1948 was a successful year on the golf course and I succeeded in winning both the President's and Captain's prizes – a solid silver, pint tankard and engine-turned silver hairbrushes. Rationing was still severe but I obtained a few extras from Mr Preston, a self-confessed rogue, who supplied us with straw and woodwool for packing. He had an extra petrol allowance so that he could go round the farms buying straw. The farmers, or their wives, were

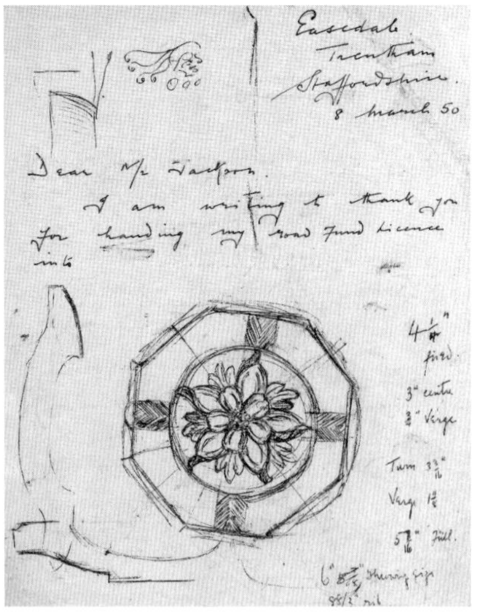

Details of an octagonal ashtray sketched on a waste piece of notepaper. This was my first break from all thrown production and sold well.

pleased to get decorated china (export only). The manufacturers were pleased to get eggs and poultry. Everyone was happy.

Life moved smoothly from the 1940s into the 1950s. Officialdom with its rationing, controls and form-filling, was a way of life. In May 1949, I once again exhibited at the B.I.F. and was invited to a dinner at the Mansion House on the occasion of its opening. The Right Honourable Harold Wilson, O.B.E., M.P. (who became Prime Minister in 1964) was in the chair. Overseas buyers flocked to the North Stafford Hotel in Stoke, and taxi drivers earned good tips for taking them to factories with available supplies – their information source resulting from overhearing the conversations of their passengers. Senior members of the leading stores came over on public relations trips. My most distinguished visitor was Henry Morgan of Henry Morgan & Company, Montreal, an elegant figure with silver-white hair who arrived in his chauffeur driven, pale blue Rolls Royce.

I received a number of very welcome food parcels from grateful customers, notably The Hon. W.C. Woodward of Woodward's Stores, Vancouver; O.B. Allan of Vancouver; Bartlett Morgan of Morgan's of Montreal and Emerson

Factory promotional colour leaflet of a range of Moorcroft pots, an experiment in contemporary advertising by Macaulay, 1952.

Moorcroft

Pottery Lamp Bases

The lamp bases illustrated on this page are made primarily for export by Moorcroft Ltd. Most striking is the delicate shading of the floral motifs from pale pink to deep purple or midnight blue against a base colour of soft green or deep blue. The shading is obtained by the fusion of one material into another at a very high temperature.

The bases are made individually by hand on the throwing machine and the decoration is applied entirely by hand.

A page from *Pottery and Glass*, May 1953, for lamp bases made for Elliott and Spear, forerunners of a substantial business.

Nichols of London, Ontario. The latter had built up a very successful wholesale business and was proud of the fact that he had started life in Longton, carrying warehouse baskets for 2s 6d a week. He had become very friendly with Harold Plant of Tuscan China (R.H. & S.L. Plant) and went to Canada to sell his wares which became the foundation of his business.

Three events dominated 1951. The Festival of Britain, peppered with good Anglo Saxon names like Fritz Müller (Council of Industrial Design) and the Hungarian designer, Mischa Black. My second daughter, Sheila, was born on the 19th April, once more as planned even to the extent of arriving on the birthday of her grandfather, Andrew Blakely. I parted with my Rover 10 in favour of the much larger Rover 75, an entirely new model incorporating interior heating. A condition of purchase was to sign an undertaking not to sell it for at least twelve months. The black market price of a new car sold 'second-hand' was double the list price.

Involved with work for the Festival of Britain, was a photographic and public relations partnership of two young men, McLeish and Macaulay. The latter persuaded me to take him on as my advertising agent and he injected some new life into our publicity. Against my better judgement, I was persuaded by representatives of the Board of Trade, because it was Coronation year and I had a Royal Appointment, to exhibit at the 1953 B.I.F. I entrusted the design of my stand to Macaulay who did it with some skill and at considerable expense. It was not a success. Overseas buyers preferred to come to the factory and home buyers were influenced by the beginning of what I named *The House and Garden* era, or the period of the anodised wastepaper basket (red, black or emerald green). This trend depressed our home sales throughout the rest of the 1950s. Our association with Macaulay ended in 1953 when his plans became over ambitious and even had results justified the extra cost, we could never have met the demand. Running the factory continued to absorb most of my energy at the expense of creative activity. The situation was accentuated by the fact that many of our overseas customers placed their orders for 'assorted designs' indicating merely a preference for background colours, of which blue was still the favourite. This considerably diminished the incentive to create new flower motifs, especially when there were so many other distractions. I did however make some drawings of freesias from which I created designs for two small vases, a bowl and a coaster.

My most stimulating business contact was the annual visit from Ed Lucas, the lamp base buyer of the T. Eaton Company of Canada. To obtain the variety he required, he would often select shapes which had been discontinued or persuade me to design new ones – he encouraged me to develop my *Hibiscus* and *Bougainvillaea* designs to put new life into the collection. The ceramic bases were elaborately fitted to stand on a metal plinth with a matching finial above the shade, the whole structure being held together by a steel rod passing through a $^5/_8$ins hole in the top and bottom. They were sold mainly in the Fine Art Department of Eaton's Toronto store. Ed's trip took him all over Europe buying electrical goods and one year he told me that he had discovered just the right fittings for the previous year's shipment. He found a designer in Paris, a bronze worker in Barcelona, and the final assembly was to take place in Toronto. While on his travels he used to select the odd special item for his personal use. In central

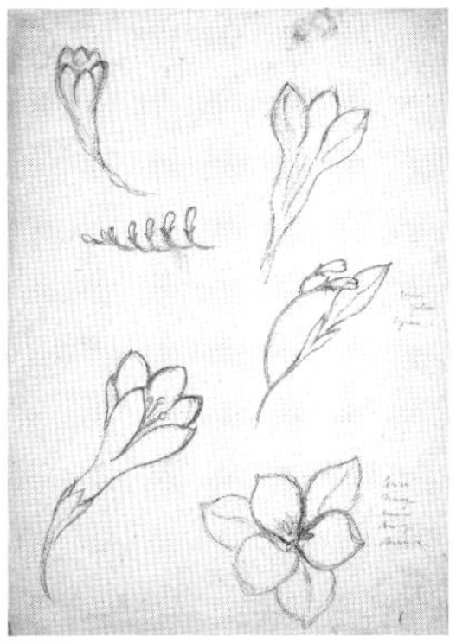
Exploratory drawings for the new *Freesia* design, 1954-55.

Europe he saw a fine cut glass decanter, just right for his sideboard and asked for it to be included in the shipment. It was. However, when he unpacked it, he found a $^5/_8$ins hole in the bottom, beautifully drilled and polished in accordance with standard specifications for lamp bases!

To a considerable extent, the limited number of new designs was offset by my production of *flambé* which provided a kaleidoscopic flow of individual pieces of which no two could be the same. A customer approached me and said that he had a very particular lady client who wanted six matching fruit plates in *Autumn Leaves flambé*. I knew that he would not accept 'no' for an answer so I listed clear conditions: delivery would take two years as I would have to make one hundred plates, from which his client could select the six nearest to a perfect match; and he would buy the remaining ninety-four if I could not sell them immediately. I was saved the trouble!

One advantage of *flambé* firing was that many a poorly coloured piece could be made brilliant by putting it through the kiln. Sometimes a paintress would pick up such a piece and, finding her mark on the back, proudly claim that she had coloured it. I did not have the heart to disillusion her. By the use of more black oxide of silver, as opposed to copper, I increased the proportion of chartreuse yellow and green which accentuated the richness of the red and darker colours. *Flambé* was bought by customers who appreciated the unique characteristics of each piece and was sold in Canada, America, South Africa, Australia and New Zealand. The Australians were keen admirers but we could only supply a fraction of their demands. When visiting the factory, one Australian customer adopted an aggressive tone, declaring that he had a complaint. Fearing the worst, I asked why. 'I object to being dragged from my bed at 6.00am to look at it. Before I left my wife did just that, because she insisted that I should see the brilliance of the early morning sun on a *flambé* vase in our drawing room!'

A display of Moorcroft in the showroom of E.S. Ranson, our Australian agents in Sydney until the 1960s.

In 1952, Mr Geoffrey Lloyd, the Minister of Fuel and Power, visited the factory. He politely showed his interest in the craftsmanship of handmade pottery, directing only a wry smile at our antiquated heating appliances in the form of cast iron stove pots, even more primitive than those used in railway waiting rooms. He also had his photograph taken while looking inside a bottle-oven. These were rapidly disappearing owing to the Clean Air Act and the extra efficiency of tunnel ovens. Tunnel ovens had a throughput

The Minister of Fuel and Power, Geoffrey Lloyd M.P., watching Harry Bailey throwing a pot, November 1952.

Left, Jack Pollecoff of Russian extraction, was a great character and served his time as Mayor. He owned a china, furniture and fashion shop in Pwllheli. Centre, sketch for a four-inch Coronation bowl with trial sketches for component motifs. Right, my sketches of vase shapes, bottom right is an old shape in a new size, 1955.

of thousands of dozens per week. Our need was for something far smaller, which we did not find until 1956.

Another visit that year was from two members of the Central Office of Information, complete with bowler hats and briefcases, who were making a survey of the pottery industry. They showed commendable interest and had some very good photographs taken but were quite at a loss when they reached the handling shop where Fred Ashley was sticking the spouts and handles on teapots. On the workbench they saw a square block of plaster with about one hundred small recesses in it. 'What is that?' asked one. 'It's a bit mould,' said Fred. 'And what is it used for?' 'It makes the bits what you stick in the teapot to hold the lid on,' said Fred. No further comment.

The King died and the coronation of Queen Elizabeth was duly arranged for June 1953. Commemorative pieces have always been a feature of the pottery industry and I felt that I must produce something to mark the occasion. I designed a beaker and a small bowl. I had the beaker made in a shape and size based on a lager glass so that Customs and Excise could not define it as a vase as this would have attracted a high rate of purchase tax. The two pieces were shown on a television programme at the mercy of a fashion-conscious presenter named Jeanne Heal who dismissed them with condescending comments that they were 'too traditional'.

Fred Ashley, the handler, photographed for the Central Office of Information.

Throughout this period, I had a cordial relationship with Liberty & Co. Although direct contact was restricted to the annual meeting of the company, held in their boardroom early in December, I always received an invitation to have lunch with their directors before the meeting. This was served in their private dining room which was reached from the main store through a door concealed in an oak-panelled wall. The lunch was attended on occasion by Captain Ivor Stewart Liberty (who had an unusual taste for drinking straight gin and water), Alwyn Lasenby, Harold Blackmore, W.H. Dorrell, Hilary Blackmore (who specialised in Liberty fabrics) and Arthur Stewart Liberty who succeeded Alwyn Lasenby as a director of W. Moorcroft Ltd. Being December, mince pies were served and I learned the technique of opening the pie and adding neat brandy from the decanter which was passed around the table. After an excellent meal, we retired to the boardroom for our meeting. Harold Blackmore joined us 'in attendance' although he had no authority over W. Moorcroft Ltd. I made this clear when he was expressing an emphatic view, by turning to Alwyn Lasenby and saying, 'Mr Lasenby you are a director of our company, may I have the answer from you?' It did not matter a great deal because with equal voting power of shares, I had the casting vote. In order to attend this meeting I made a day trip to London. I caught an early train from Stafford on which breakfast was served and returned on the 5.20 from Euston taking a seat in the dining car, where there was time for afternoon tea, a cocktail and a full evening meal (seven and sixpence) between Euston and Stafford.

By the mid-1950s, the removal of controls had been accelerated by the election of a Conservative government. Supplies of merchandise were gradually catching up with demand and it was once more necessary to look for orders.

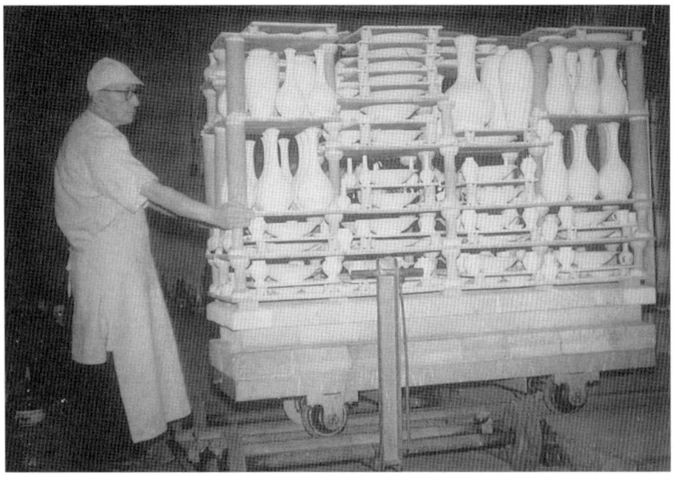

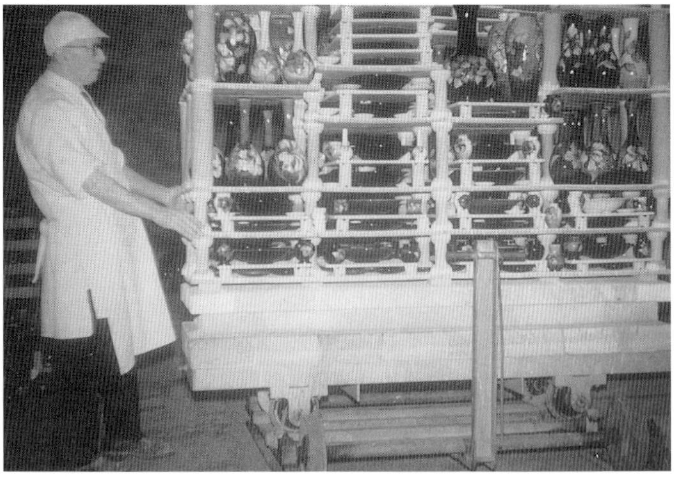

Jack Hill, dipper and fireman, placing a truck of decorated ware, all white after being dipped in glaze, into the kiln; the same truck comes out after firing, 1956.

For several years a Toy Fair had been held in Harrogate which increasingly developed into a general Gift Fair and in 1955, several pottery manufacturers had applied for space which had become very limited. The organisers, Trade Promotion Services, headed by Elkan Simons recognised the potential and moved the Fair to Blackpool as the International Gifts Fair. This later became universally known as the Blackpool Fair. It opened in 1956 and was housed in the Winter Gardens, the Talbot Hall (an early multi-storey car park) and various hotels. The pottery industry enjoyed outstanding accommodation at the Imperial Hotel. Simplicity was the order of the day and hotel rooms were used instead of expensive display stands. The Fair lasted for one week and my comment on the result was that in comparison with the old B.I.F. in London, we had done twice the business, in half the time, at a quarter of the cost.

Pressure was increasing to dispense with coal firing in accordance with the Clean Air Act. We had three bottle-ovens, one for biscuit firing, the firing of the clayware at 1120°-1130°C, and two for glost firing at 1080°C. Owing to our limited output, we needed something much smaller than the tunnel kilns which were in general use in the industry. I was fortunate to be introduced to Ted Litherland who was a specialist in firing processes and owned the company bearing his name. He had designed an intermittent electric kiln which might have been custom made for our requirements as it had the right capacity and could fire anything from enamel temperatures to china biscuit. As well as an electronic control panel, it had spy holes in the kiln doors which allowed the temperature to be checked visually using the thermo-bars to which my fireman had been accustomed in the bottle-oven. Electric firing was more expensive than gas, but firing represented a very small percentage of our production costs and electricity offered the great advantage of complete freedom from fumes which might have affected our colours.

In August 1956, while the factory was closed for two week's holiday, one of our bottle-ovens was demolished and the site cleared. A twin-chambered electric kiln for the glost firing was installed and the first firing took place, most appropriately, on 5th November, but there were no fireworks. The result was perfect. When Ted Litherland saw the first truck come out he was staggered by the result. By normal industrial procedure the ware went into the kiln white (covered in glaze) and came out white ready for on-glaze decorating. With our colours already fired into the biscuit, the ware went into the kiln white and came out a blaze of colour. We continued to use coal for biscuit firing until 1960, when we demolished a second bottle-oven to make room for an electric kiln. We kept the third bottle-oven on account of its link with the past and its graceful appearance. The previous autumn I had been invited to visit a customer in Norfolk. As I drove through the wheat-growing area, I passed a number of corn mills which were housed in rather monotonous low buildings except for one which had a beautifully restored windmill and stood out from all the rest. I felt that the same would apply to our single-storey factory. I had continued using coal for biscuit firing because of uncertainty of the effect on the colours which we used for decoration. I felt reassured when I learned that Minton's had made their last coal firing about the same time. Although our productions were totally different, we were both specialists in our different ways.

I find it difficult to write about the details of my home life in the 1950s. Highlights of happiness and a successful marriage were overshadowed by problems arising from events. Soon after we were married, Molly's parents had a bitter separation which alienated her completely from her mother. In 1952, her father, to whom she was completely devoted, died in the course of a day from a heart attack at the early age of sixty-one. Her cousin, David Blakely, was murdered by the nightclub hostess, Ruth Ellis, who was the last woman to be hanged in Britain. Molly was dedicated to perfection: perfection in her personal appearance, her home and her children. Sadly, some inner turmoil, which I was never able to define, gradually estranged her from the outside world and Easedale became an area of almost total seclusion, without visitors, young or old.

The *Hedgevine* was on one vase shape with three different background colours including yellow and in only two sizes. Blue vase 12ins, 1960 (see page 73).

Below, *Sunray* was produced with an orange glaze on our full range of tableware shapes. Intended for firing at 20°F below our normal temperature, results were inclined to be erratic, especially on flat pieces on which it often erupted like volcanic hot springs, adding fuel to my father's Monday morning arguments with the fireman, c1933-1940.

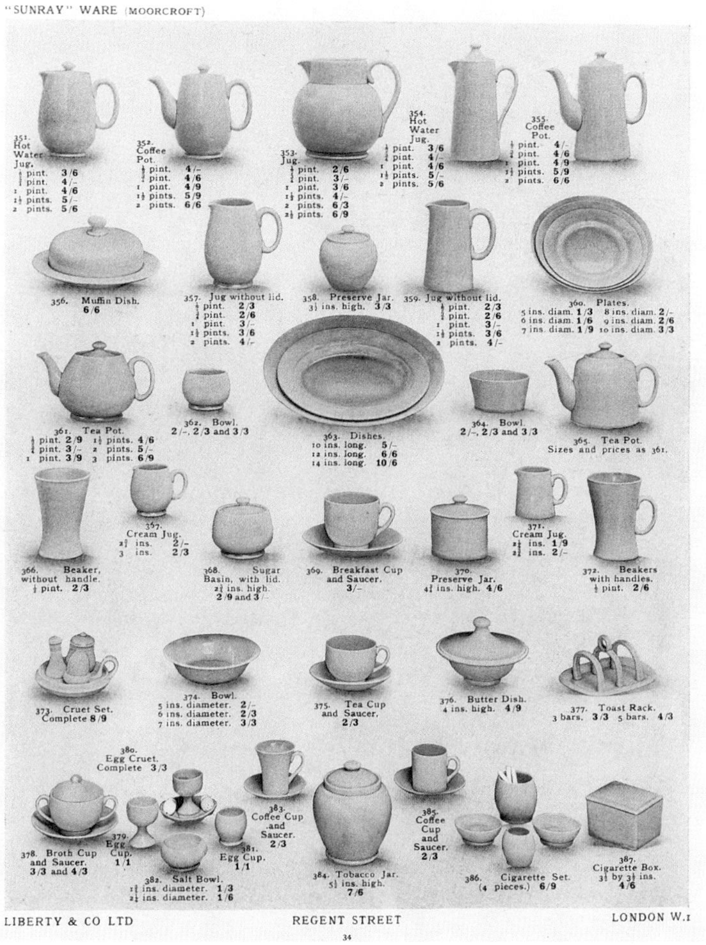

Cottages in Newbold on Avon, June 1933. I painted this while a member of the Sketching Club at Rugby School.

Canal tunnel, Newbold on Avon, May 1933. Described as 'unfinished', I can remember the blue and yellow effect creeping in as I worked on it in the fading light in my study towards the end of the day.

My father's punch bowl used by Liz for serving curry at parties, diameter 14ins.

Left, my first design while still at school. A vase with imperial motifs based on postage stamps to commemorate the Silver Jubilee of George V and Queen Mary, my father's signature on the base, 1935.

Above, pipe knocker ashtray 'Natural *flambé*'. Part of a group of smoker's accessories I designed for T. Eaton Co., of Canada, 1938-9.

Perfume bottles which I engineered from a glass sample sent over from America in about 1939. Turning the stoppers on the lathe from a solid lump of clay and making them fit was quite tricky.

Orchid and *Spring Flowers* designs on an ivory background. I designed the vertical shape as a change from the normally curvaceous style of Moorcroft vases, late 1950s.

Midnight blue *Orchid flambé* 10ins plate, and rectangular box of my design with lighter *flambé* colouring, 1950-55.

Autumn Leaves flambé, 12ins. A successful colour mutation in the kiln without my later addition of silver, dated 1946.

Autumn Leaves Green. This was originally intended solely as a basis for *Autumn Leaves flambé*. It was just beginning to be sold on its own merit when I started at the factory in 1935 and was entered in the packing book as 'Leaf less Flambé'.

Orchid design on 12¼ins bowl with new yellow as a background colour. A perfect example of using my father's design for a different effect, 1957.

Tiger Lily flambé bowl, $12^1/_2$ins, 1964-65.

Lily flambé vase, 14ins, dated 1962. I remember sketching this holding a lily in one hand and a fine brush in the other to make the drawing on the clay.

Tiger Lily plate, 10ins, on ivory background, c1965. There were about six of these made.

Tiger Lily powder bowl lid, 1937. My design, signed by my father!

Watercolour of *Tiger Lily* painted in my study at Rugby when I was seventeen, dated 8.10.34.

Collection of *Bougainvillea* showing a variety of colour and interpretation. The 12ins lamp base was made for Eaton's of Canada, 1952-1960.

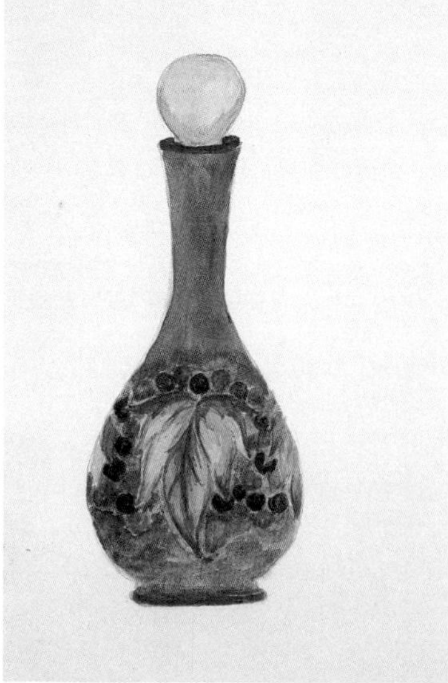

Above, *Autumn Leaves flambé* vase adapted as a container for lotions in Austin Reed's hair salon (see page 23).

Left, a *Maple Leaf* lamp base which I designed for Eaton's of Canada who had sent pressed leaves, 1969.

Wild Rose designed for Liberty but produced only as prototypes, 1980.

My only Christmas plate. Commissioned by Woodward's Stores of Vancouver but not taken up as they required an item available in a larger quantity and at a lower price. I chose *Poinsettia* as a motif more suited to Moorcroft than Santa Claus and holly, 1967.

Pencil drawing for *Poinsettia* Christmas plate, 1967.

Columbine in a rare variety of *flambé* colours which are dependant on the background colours, on the application of silver or copper and the number of firings, 1955-60.

In the 1950s I designed the lamp base on the left with a green background and used the simple layout of the design for the basis of the extended range on the ivory background in the early 1980s. Oval bowl, 1971.

Ink drawing of *Hibiscus* for Ted Takarada of Yokahama. Above, 'Best Wishes' plate, 1980.

Right, the first *Columbine*, dated 1947, the vase 7ins, footed bowl 4½ins.

A group of *Clematis* pieces drawn with a differently shaped flower and composition of design to break away from my father's style, 1959-60.

Freesia coaster, vase and small bowl which I designed in the 1950s. The design is often confused with my father's *African Lily* and also *Spring Flowers* which included freesia-type flowers without naming them.

Candy boxes: the two at the back, about 6ins diameter, were made under my supervision from an American sample, 1938-39. The one at the front had been made with a plain convex lid until 1937, when a knob was added at the request of a Canadian buyer which dramatically increased the sale of this shape. The boxes had to be described as 'candy boxes' because powder boxes attracted a far higher duty.

Clematis flambé vase, 8ins. The flower and bud motif were designed in the late 1950s.

A group of *Clematis* pieces. The oval tray signed 19.12.70 was taken hot from the kiln just in time to take as a sample of the new range of all oval pieces on my transatlantic trip on 1st January, 1971.

Five special pieces of *Hibiscus flambé*, 1954-1965. The beaker vase has a 'brandy flame', an iridescence which came just before overfiring. The bowls show the yellow obtained from silver oxide – effects which can never be duplicated.

First pencil sketch for *Hibiscus*, 1949. I can remember making the sketch lying on the floor at home with the pressed flowers beside me.

This *Hibiscus flambé* plate and ginger jar illustrates the 'freak' factor of the brandy flame effect, c1960.

Right, *Hibiscus flambé* vase. Exotic tropical colours produced in the *flambé* kiln. The red of the flower accentuated by the chartreuse yellow and green background, my most treasured vase since 1949 (see cover). I made a few of these for ships of the Cunard Line sailing from Liverpool to the Caribbean. The shape of the foot enabled them to be clipped to a table to compensate for the movement of the ship.

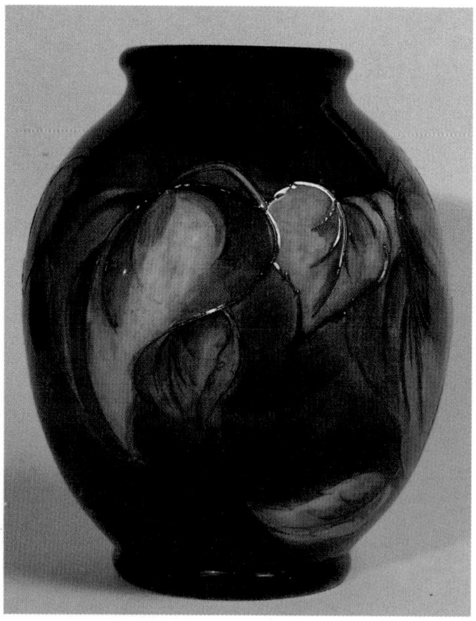

Far left, *Poplar Leaves* design on ivory, similar to the piece I gave to Princess Margaret for a wedding present, 1960.

Left, *Poplar Leaves flambé* vase, similar to the one sold to my special client in Madrid (see page 73).

Below, rough pastel sketch for colouring of *Poplar* design (see page 73).

Leaves in the Wind. 'My glorious failure' (see page 73).

Maize, 1976. Proposed lamp base design for Eaton's of Canada, but declined as it was a vegetable!

Pansy Nouveau, 1970. Designed specially for Ebeling and Reuss, our distributors in the U.S.A. Discontinued, Autumn 1972.

Jug and ashtray made for Marston's Brewery (described on their letterhead as 'The Brewery Burton-on-Trent'). Designed from a drawing of a hop, about 500 of each were made.

Rhododendron vase, $7\frac{1}{2}$ins. This was a prototype which I designed in about 1964 but never put into production.

Caribbean design, 1958 to early 1960s. An idle observer of the tankard on the right commented that nobody was in the boat. I told him that they had been frightened by the leaping fish and had jumped out on the other side.

Marine design, 1960. Note exotic fish inspired by my wife, Liz, on centre vase.

Marine drawings.

A very unusual group. I drew the *Maple Leaf* on the left from maple leaves sent from the Appalachians. The *Allamander* on the box is a flower from Bermuda. The *Orchid* 'Laelia Autumnalis' was taken from the *Year Book of the Royal Horticultural Society*. The bowl on the right shows my original *Tiger Lily* design.

My interpretation of my father's *African Lily* in rich *flambé* colours accentuated with silver.

A new 5ins vase shape I designed in the late 1950s with my drawing of my father's *African Lily*.

A group of *Wild Arum flambé*, an ideal design for utilising the *flambé* effect through the decorative shape of the leaves, early 1960s. The 8ins bowl on oxblood – a unique piece.

Wild Arum flambé bowl, 9½ins. An outstanding example of the golden yellow.

A dramatic interpretation of the *Wild Arum* with midnight blue *flambé*, 1962-63.

A group of *Wild Arum* which originated from the search for a motif for the lamp base on the left, made in a variety of shapes and colours including the use of the leaf on its own.

A group of *Anemone* pieces ranging from my father's design, far left, in one of my rare *flambé* colours – to my latest style of drawing far right, 1989. The yellow vase is a design showing my breakaway from the wreath type of decoration, 1989. The jardiniere shows one of my father's drawings which I reproduced on a white background, c1961. This popular motif has been in production in different styles for over sixty years.

Preliminary design for my first year plate commissioned by Dave Bradshaw of Stratford, Ontario, and my watercolour for the year plate of 1985.

Coral Hibiscus on green and ivory, an escape from the blues and pinks, 1970 (see page 80).

Two of a group of six shapes, backstamped 1872-1972, each produced in three different colours to commemorate the centenary of my father's birth. They were limited to production during the centenary year and ranged from 80 to 200 of each item.

Hibiscus vase, 12ins, on ivory background commissioned by Allders of Croydon, 1964. I designed the ashtray with rests $1\frac{1}{8}$ins long so that a cigarette would burn out, before falling off the tray.

Hibiscus jardiniere on ivory, 1960. A very good example of the earlier drawings incorporating the bud which was eliminated with the restyling for *Coral Hibiscus*, 1968-69. *Hibiscus* candy box on green, 1961-62.

A group of *Bermuda Lily*, one of my favourite designs, 1971-72 (see page 81).

Above, watercolour of *Bermuda Lily*, 1972.

Right, looking for something new in the late 1970s, I used the *Bermuda Lily* drawings with a deep brown background (a mixture of half brown and half green pigments) and called it *Jungle Brown Lily*.

Eastern Lily is a version of *Bermuda Lily* which arose from a request from Canada for the design on an ivory background, 1975.

Bermuda Lily oval box and coaster, 4$^{1}/_{2}$ins, on turquoise slip, 1971. Examples of a few experimental pieces prior to adopting the olive green background.

Magnolia oval boxes, 1975-76. The first prototype was produced in 1975.

Ivory Magnolia which I designed about two years after the launch of the new design in 1976. The candlestick on the right was one of my 'post-retirement' pieces, added to the range in 1992.

Watercolour on typing paper, a colour plan for *Magnolia*, 1975.

Left, *Purple Magnolia* vase, 5ins, designed specially for Australia with limited sales in this country. The yellow ground was my personal choice but not widely marketed, late 1970s.

Magnolia, 1976-77. The 'shocking pink' of the flowers produced a completely new effect on the dark blue background.

A group of miniature vases first produced on the throwing wheel, 1964. Later made by casting, including rare *flambé* examples.

Mugs made for my family: Jean 1953, Sheila 1954, Sara 1960, Liz 1961 and my granddaughter, Hannah, 1994.

A 12ins plate presented to me in 1985 to commemorate fifty years at Moorcroft. Each flower taken from my designs bears the mark of a different paintress.

Presentation plate, 14ins, made for my retirement in 1987. *Freesias* were the flower of the moment.

Watercolours for my butterfly motifs, 1984.

Wild Arum vase, and two with butterfly motifs, 7ins, 1984.

My 'Monday, Tuesday, Wednesday' *Tulip* design (see page 90). First produced in 1985 and reintroduced with pink and yellow flowers for Dave Simmons in Canada, late 1986.

Watercolour on typing paper – a colour guide for a late *Wild Arum* vase, 1986.

Campanula designed for Churchill China, 1985. Produced for the lower-price market with the design engraved in the mould. Vase on the left was a tube-lined prototype, dated 31.5.85.

Group of mugs: *Thistle*, *Bluebell*, *Daffodil*, *Geranium*, *Campanula*. Designed for Churchill China, 1985-86.

Group of *Geranium* pieces sketched while on holiday in Crete. The vase on the left, 6ins, dated 11.10.84.

After the Storm, 20ins, which I designed specially for the 1997 Centenary.

Jackson of Bradford opened their account on allocations of export rejects after the war and became loyal stockists during the years that followed. From the late 1940s Mrs Jackson was a regular visitor to the factory, a Junoesque figure whom I nicknamed with affection 'Diamond Lil'.

Photograph of popular shapes with their shape numbers sent out to selected customers, c1955.

Left, demolition of the first glost oven at the east end, August 1956.

Bottom left, the front of the factory, showing the field area and saggars cleared from the biscuit oven stacked against the wall, before work started on developing the factory shop, early 1971.

Bottom right, the new look. The saggars have been used to build the rose garden, the field converted into a car park and the factory painted the colour of Californian sand with the new Moorcroft sign to complete the picture, 1971.

Flambé kilns at the west end, coming down, 1971. I was sent for by the steeplejack so I could see how he was knocking the bricks out with his gloved hand. 'It's a wonder it hasn't ruddy blown down!' he said.

The *flambé* kiln as I had always known it, showing the fire mouths. I used to lick my finger and hold it up to see which way the wind was blowing. From the north they burned too fast, from the south, too slow.

Rear of the factory immediately after demolition of the kilns. The shape of the lean-to roof around the *flambé* kiln can be seen clearly on the wall and the door connecting the kilns with the *flambé* room, 1971.

The same view a month later, the 'shard ruck' on the left has been levelled and turfed, the path relaid and the walls repainted the colour of Californian sand.

Molly's Death and Life in Limbo

Sleep was hard to come by and I had a lacklustre approach to my work...

Summer holidays brought a spark of relief with some sociable life amongst strangers. For five consecutive years we spent our summer holiday at the Marine Hotel in Criccieth where the proprietors had children of the same age as ours and the year that Sheila was in a pram, gave us the services of their nanny. In 1955 and 1956 we went to the Royal Gate House Hotel in Tenby where it was still customary to change for dinner. Apart from a complete wardrobe of day and evening wear for herself, Molly also took twenty-two frocks for the girls, then aged five and seven, to last them for a fortnight. We had two wonderful holidays in Tenby, but 1956 was to be the last. Two weeks after arriving home, Molly experienced the first sign of trouble. After six weeks of traumatic and contradictory diagnoses by various consultants, she died on the 23rd October, 1956, at the Queen Elizabeth Hospital in Birmingham, from a tumour on the brain. She was thirty-seven.

Jean, Molly, myself and Sheila on holiday in Tenby, 1956.

My life went into neutral. I survived with a housekeeper, a daily help and some sterling assistance from my sister, Beatrice, and my stepmother, Hazel, with whom we had not associated for years owing to a total rift between Molly and Hazel, about which I prefer to make no comment other than I had every reason to remain totally loyal to my wife. My only criticism of my sister was her tendency to become the all-embracing 'Auntie Bea' and getting the children wild with excitement – which, as they had not been accustomed to such behaviour, I compared to taking a cork from a champagne bottle too quickly. I moved Jean and Sheila from their school near Stone to Chaucer House on the outskirts of Longton which was much nearer home. Here I received incredible support and kindness from two women who also had children at the school. Margaret Brown, who had sat next to me at Field House School in the 1920s, and Gladys Johnson, the wife of Basil, a director of Johnson Bros., the potters. They just took over the girls during the day, and I knew that they could not be in safer hands. Life had to go on, but I used to say that I was pushing the factory rather than running it.

Anglesey Cliffs, 1957.

In 1957 I had to plan a seaside holiday for the girls and a friend of mine recommended Trearddur Bay in Anglesey. Beatrice volunteered her support to provide the vital female assistance required to cope with two small girls on holiday, and I made a reservation at the Trearddur Bay Hotel for two weeks in August (14 guineas a week full board and special terms for children). This proved to be a significant decision.

Trearddur had a large sandy bay and three small bays all within a mile. The furthest bay, Porth y Castell, was most inviting and after a morning on 'big bay' we went there, armed with my luxury picnic case which the hotel had filled with an afternoon tea. We settled down on some comfortable rocks. However, the Manson family had sat on these for years, and we were intruders. Mrs Manson, a homely-looking woman had a Staffordshire Bull Terrier, commendably kept on a lead, a teenage daughter called Janet and, with her, a lovely girl called Elisabeth Thomas. We engaged in conversation and I offered Elisabeth a piece of cake, which she accepted. (Forty years on and we are still happily married. Little did we know!)

Porth y Castell with Holyhead Mountain in the background, 1957.

During 1957-1958, I was largely in a state of limbo. Even with the help of sleeping pills and a strong nightcap, sleep was hard to come by and I had a lacklustre approach to my work. I was very much aware of the need for new designs and experimented with one or two existing motifs on a turquoise slip. I also designed a *Dianthus* motif which never went further than about fifty small vases. It seemed that I lacked the confidence or motivation to promote my designs though a more successful effort was my own interpretation of the *Clematis*, drawn from a multi-petalled variety with a flower and half-open bud forming a spray, but even this appeared on only two vases and two bowls. About this time an important item was added to our productions in the form of lamp bases designed specially for the home market so that they could be fitted up without the plinths universally used in north America. They were made at the instigation of a firm of lamp base manufacturers in Liverpool called Specialities who placed orders for fifty of each item in sizes much smaller than those made for north America, ranging from six inches to nine inches high. These were ideally suited to placing on the trucks in our new kiln and made a very useful addition to our output, which was in need of new designs.

My new interpretation of the *Clematis* design, c1958.

I had a timely jolt from a great character, Charlie White, who owned Robert Hogg & Co., of Belfast. He bought a lot of seconds from us at half price or less and wrote me a letter suggesting that I should invest in a wheelbarrow and a hammer. Anything unsaleable I should smash and he would buy the rest. Charlie said that he never promoted anything at half price but instead, two for the price of one and claimed that he was doing a service to the young people of Ulster by providing betrothal presents at prices they could afford. I needed to break away from the influence of my father which still dominated the factory and, though the measures were more extreme than I was prepared to accept, the general message was correct. Charlie was an extraordinary character who was best summed up by my secretary when I asked her whether she would like to work for him. 'I think Mr White's secretary must be a leprechaun!' she replied.

An early attempt at coloured publicity showing the ivory background and the new yellow, 1959-60.

At the Blackpool Fair 1958, I showed an all-yellow piece for the first time – a slender twelve inch vase with purple clematis on a lemon yellow background. It caused quite a sensation. This was an entirely new yellow, both in colour and physical quality. The yellow used previously had played only a secondary part in the decoration as it would not stand up to the higher temperature of the first firing and had to be painted on the biscuit. The new yellow was supplied to us by the colour manufacturers, Harrisons of Hanley, who were always willing to help with technical problems. Originally, it had been formulated as a stain to withstand the high temperatures in firing sanitary ware but ground to our specifications, it was ideal for freehand painting. Use of this new colour enabled me to include a bright yellow flower in my *Hibiscus* decoration and for the first time, it stood clearly apart from the other designs. The yellow flower remained a feature of this design until the end of the 1960s. As time went on I made extensive use of this yellow as a background colour not only for my *Hibiscus* but also with some of my father's designs, notably the *Orchid*, which gave them a completely new look.

At about this time and quite by accident, I created the *Wild Arum* design. One of my lamp base customers chose a tall bottle-shaped vase, which had not been decorated previously. It needed something different and drawing on the clay with a brush as usual, I made a series of sweeping curves which reminded me of a flower that I used to see in the hedgerow as a child. I looked up its details in a book on wild flowers and then found it growing in profusion at Chebsey, a very rural place about fifteen miles from home, where I discovered the spotted variety which added just that extra touch of interest.

In the spring of 1958 my sister persuaded me to accompany her for a week in Copenhagen, where she had arranged to meet some friends. I knew that the Royal Copenhagen factory was at least partially open to the public and I wrote to them telling them of my forthcoming visit. With great courtesy, they took me on a private tour.

It was an education to see the superb ceramic figures which rarely, if ever, were seen in the general retail market. In Copenhagen there was a permanent exhibition on the lines of the Design Centre in the Haymarket and I found it ironic, though because of their austere views on design, not entirely surprising, that their representation of Royal Copenhagen was plain white tableware. During the 1950s I had been told by a would-be adviser that I should seriously consider following the example of Scandinavian design. I declined on the grounds that it would not be Moorcroft, that I could not hope to produce it as well as the Scandinavians did, and I would be joining the end of a long line of other imitators.

In August we returned to Trearddur Bay for another family holiday. We arrived on a lovely evening so I put the hood down on my Ford Convertible and went for a drive around the bays. As I drove slowly alongside the sea, I saw ahead two pairs of female legs belonging to Elisabeth and her friend Janet. (I had seen Elisabeth once during the year when my sister tactfully invited her to come over for a night at Glendair so that I could show her the factory.) Elisabeth was staying with the Mansons, as in the previous year, and I realised immediately how much I had been looking forward to seeing her again. We soon discovered a mutual interest in the *Daily Telegraph* crossword, which allowed discreet proximity on the beach and, by some strange coincidence, nearly every evening there would be a reason for Elisabeth to come to the hotel for suitable refreshment. The holiday ended and we maintained contact in writing on the pretext of discussing ideas for new designs. Elisabeth had considerable artistic talent and had won a major award while still at school.

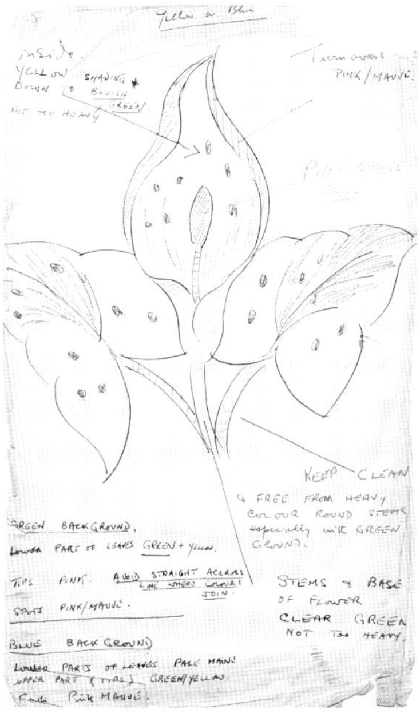

My instructions for colouring the *Wild Arum* decoration, 1958.

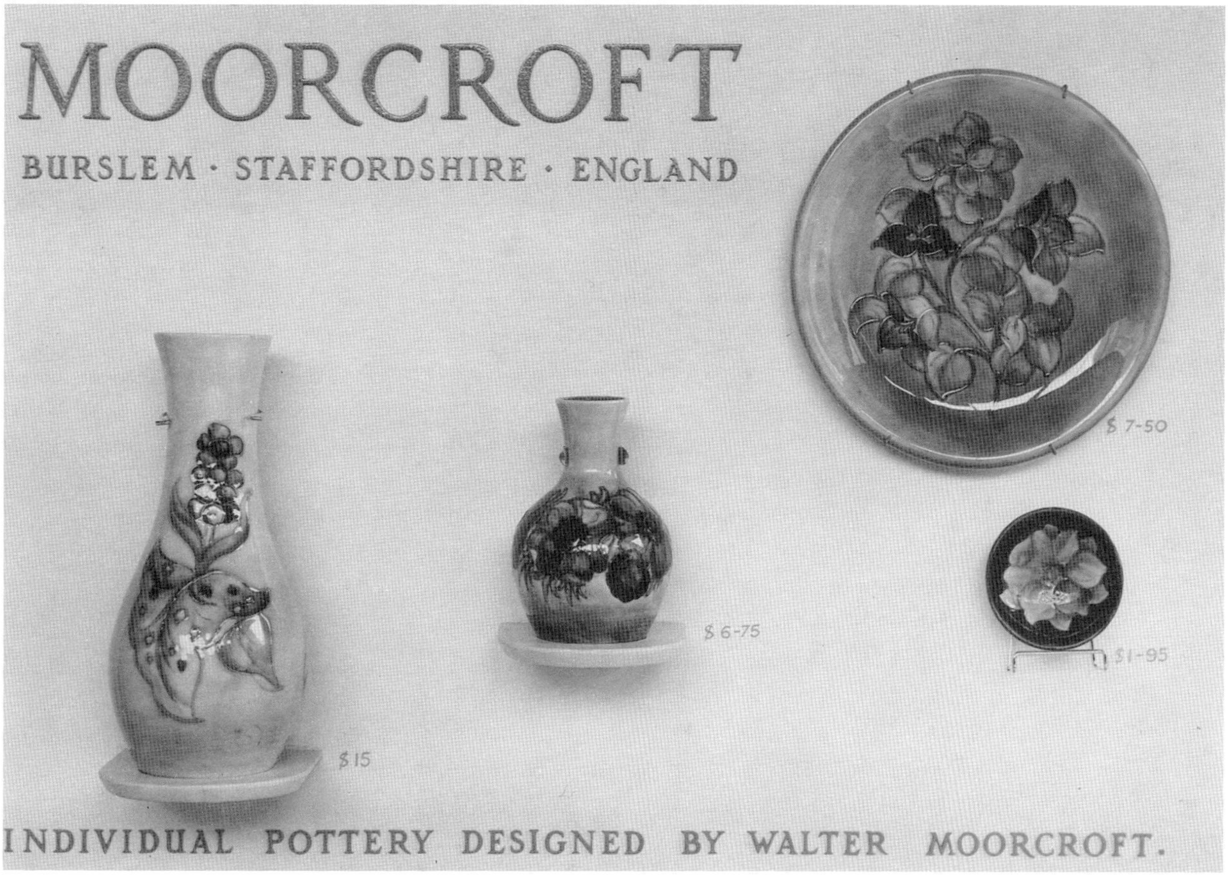

A panel of Moorcroft pottery displayed at The Chicago Fair 1959, picturing the *Wild Arum* vase on the far left, but without the backing of a distributor it made little impact.

Elisabeth

A New Life

Elisabeth became Liz…she took an immediate interest in the factory, getting to know everybody…

Emotions were fermenting like a heady wine and by the end of November I knew that action must be taken. Elisabeth lived in Mansfield so I arranged to make a business trip to nearby Nottingham on 1st December and asked if I could take her out to dinner in the evening. She accepted my invitation and we went to the White Post at Southwell, ten miles away. Before we set off I gave her a bracelet as a present which would, at least, be a souvenir if all else failed. We enjoyed an excellent meal and on the journey back to Mansfield I pulled into a layby and asked her to marry me. She said, 'yes!' We returned to her home to break the news to her mother who was in the bath when we arrived, and came downstairs in great confusion calling me Mr Moorhouse. I told her not to worry, as my driving licence had the same error – in those days licences were handwritten.

Elisabeth phoned her father the next morning who simply asked, 'Who to this time?' She'd had a previous engagement, various suitors and I said many times afterwards, more than half jokingly, that without my knowledge of these past experiences I would never have dared ask someone so young to marry me. We were married on St. Valentine's day, 14th February 1959. This was two days after my birthday and one day before Elisabeth's – so on our wedding day, I was forty-two and she was twenty-two. For our honeymoon I took her to Paris and Lugano, travelling by land and sea.

It was as though I had been reborn. Life had a completely new dimension. As my wife, Elisabeth became Liz. She was a sensation. Invited by the local ladies to a coffee morning, she turned up wearing my shaggy off-white golf sweater, known as my Yeti sweater, and red stockings. Liz took an immediate interest in the factory, getting to know everybody – and organised the annual film show, a social evening held in the decorating shop at the works. This consisted of a display of colour slides (still a novelty in those days) illustrating our year's activities and we finished off with tea, coffee and light refreshments which were prepared by the work people.

To quote the then Prime Minister, Harold Macmillan, the 1960s could well be called the decade of 'The wind of change'. W. Moorcroft Ltd., gained independence from Liberty's. At the 1959 annual meeting, Liberty expressed the wish to sell their shares in Moorcroft on very reasonable terms. I accepted their offer and in 1960, the legal details of reorganising the company were settled in the office of my solicitor and friend, John Moxon. My stepmother, Hazel, and sister, Beatrice, each acquired a few shares and I bought the rest. I now held five-sevenths of the shares in the company, which put me in complete control.

We fired a bottle-oven for the last time. The making of *Powder Blue Tableware* was discontinued as was throwing on the wheel and at the end of the decade in 1970, the production of *flambé* ceased. There is no doubt that the entry of Liz into my life had given me the jolt needed to

Liz and myself in Trearddur Bay, 1959.

Playing golf at Trentham with 'yeti' sweater and waterproof-windproof trousers.

A Moorcroft display in the gallery of Senor Montes in Oviedo, Spain, who bought from us regularly throughout the 1960s.

pull myself out of a state of limbo. Added to this was the valuable exchange of ideas between us; a direct example of this was my *Marine* design which was inspired by some of her drawings of exotic fish. As a result of a chance remark from a customer I started working on an ivory background, first with *Spring Flowers* then, most successfully, with *Hibiscus*. We had used a matt off-white background known as saltglaze in my father's time but this was mixed with zinc oxide which completely changed the colouring of the decoration. My *Caribbean* design was the outcome of a special commission from Trimingham's, an exclusive store in Bermuda, to provide a set of tankards with a Caribbean motif. Not having been there I had to rely on my imagination and added a few more items to make a small range for general production.

In the autumn of 1959 there was an amazing number of poplar leaves on the golf course, often concealing a ball in the middle of the fairway. These varied enormously in size and colour and I collected some to take home for drawing and as a result, produced my *Poplar* design. However, I only applied it to one large vase, of which comparatively few were made, in colour schemes of ivory, woodsmoke and *flambé*. I gave one with the ivory background painted by Marjorie Kurbanda, one of my senior paintresses, to Princess Margaret as a wedding present but, unlike her sister, the Queen, she did not send a personal acknowledgement. One of the *flambé* pieces went to a customer in Madrid who returned the following year specially to ask for another. He told me that he had kept it in his office and had been persuaded to part with it to satisfy a special client – but he had changed the price on the way down to the shop. During the 1960s we had very good customers in Madrid, Santander, Oviedo and Bilbao.

On a family outing to Chester Zoo, we found glorious yellow lilies growing in the elephant house. I managed to buy some from a florist and, to get the feeling of the flower, I held a lily in one hand and sketched it on to a vase with the other. The result was quite different from the first lily which I had done in 1946. In addition to the vase, I adapted it for a plate and a large bowl.

When visiting Jean and Sheila at school in Malvern, we would stay with my sister, Beatrice, who lived in a large flat overlooking the racecourse in Worcester. We drove for miles through the lanes of Worcestershire and Hereford where bryony was growing rampant in the hedgerows. I used this as the basis of a design which I called *Hedgevine* for a single vase in two sizes. Sadly these new pieces were only seen at the annual trade fair and without a catalogue or promotional build-up, they failed to make the impact which they possibly deserved and traditional Moorcroft continued to dominate the scene. *Leaves in the Wind* which made the greatest impact (and which I finally renamed 'My Glorious Failure'), consisted of two inverted leaves in brown and yellow on a white background. We made eight shapes which were illustrated on a small leaflet. At the Blackpool Fair it was heralded as something entirely new, in keeping with the 1960s and nearly everybody bought it, including overseas buyers. However, we had no repeat orders and I could only conclude that it was just not recognised as Moorcroft.

Putting the finishing touches to my pots displayed on the Whirligig made for me by an exhibition fitter who was also an undertaker. The shelves were threaded on a core of copper tubes. His comment was 'please don't ask me to make another!' Blackpool Fair 1959.

The Blackpool Fair 1960, still featuring *Powder Blue Tableware* and the Whirligig.

The Blackpool Fair, 1961.

Blackpool Fair 1961, the Princess Royal and I had a long conversation concerning the development of my new designs.

My Brother Joins the Company

Sara was born on the 29th December 1960...on 12th October 1965, Lise arrived

In 1962 my brother John approached me about joining the company and I agreed which, in the long term, proved to be a very good decision. After gaining his degree at Oxford, John had worked for three years with I.C.T. selling computers and punch-card systems for industrial use. This gave him valuable experience in business methods and the structure of larger companies. In 1963, John's first important job at the factory was to make a complete analysis of our sales of *Powder Blue Tableware*. Increasingly, I had been aware that the wage bill for production was rapidly catching up with the total value of sales and we had an alarming proportion of seconds. Substantial orders for these from the Canadian market had been a mainstay of our sales for years. The method of production of *Powder Blue* was extremely labour intensive. Apart from being hand-thrown each piece had to go on to the lathe twice; first to turn the shape and then, after being dipped into the blue slip, in order to remove the surplus slip from the bottom. Every spout and handle had to be dipped separately in slip. The tiny lugs that held the covers of jugs and teapots in place were individually made and Fred Ashley, the handler, told me that some pieces had to be picked up and put down twenty-eight times to complete the process. The small team of craftsmen who had produced the blue tableware for years was dwindling. Wages for their replacements were rising sharply and I found the prospect of a substantial price increase, and the possibility of a drop in standards, unacceptable and so we decided that its production must be discontinued. We had a large warehouse filled with seconds and, in order to clear it, we sold about 25,000 pieces to a factor at sixpence a piece. This gave us the first open space in the factory for years.

During the same year, the Board of Trade sponsored British participation in a Paris trade fair for the china and glass industries with the impressive sounding name, L'Exposition Internationale des Industries des Arts du Feu. It lasted for two weeks but did more to improve my knowledge of the French language than the company's bank balance. An all too frequent comment was, '*c'est jolie mais c'est trop chère*.' A French wholesaler exhibiting nearby was impressed by a group of jardinieres which I had developed the previous year but when he heard the price, his face fell and he invited me to his stand which displayed the Italian equivalent at a tenth of my price. It was, however, a stimulating experience and a challenging moment arose when I was involved, without any warning, in a brief interview on French radio concerning the

My *Fuchsia* design of 1963 which was never developed.

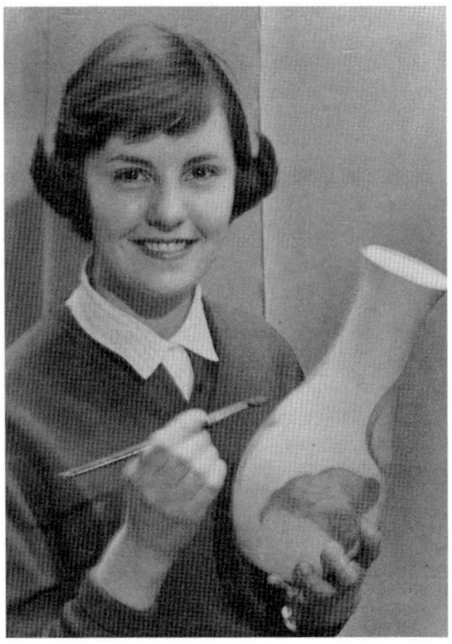

Joan Bott, a Moorcroft paintress who came second in the Pottery Queen competition of 1960. After leaving the factory, she moved to Blackpool and assisted on the Moorcroft exhibition stand at the Fair.

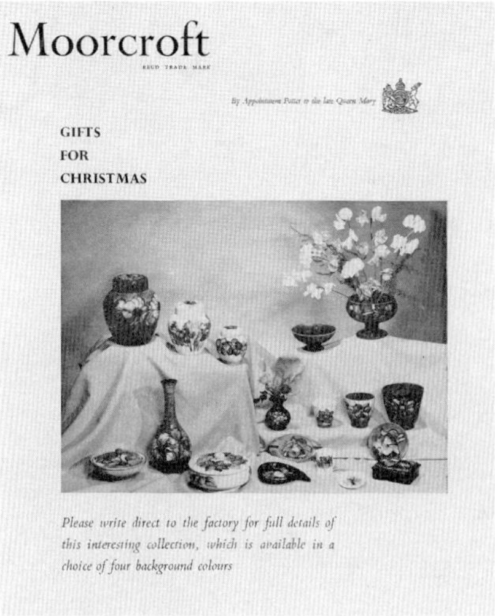

An advertisement page in *The Pottery Gazette*, September 1964.

progress of the Fair. Liz, Jean and Sheila came with me for the first week of the Fair and we stayed at a small hotel near the Madeleine. I left them to go sight-seeing during the day, and we went out together in the evenings. When the exhibition was being set up I heard a fine example of colloquial French. There was a blinding flash on the next stand and the electrician gesticulated with the comment, '*Dommage les spots sont mort*' – 'the spotlights are dead'.

In 1964 I designed a group of four miniature vases in traditional shapes but deliberately smaller than those made with detailed decorations in the early days of Moorcroft. They met with considerable success and an interesting point of sale was a glass jar filled with them like so many sweets, by the cash desk in the gift department of Jacksons of Piccadilly. In 1966 we produced our first catalogue, a small booklet printed in black and white which was greatly facilitated by the necessary reduction in our range of shapes and sizes following the end of throwing in the previous year. In my search for new ventures I designed a set of four ashtrays. These had rests 1¹/₈ins in length so that the cigarette would burn out before falling on to the table.

My last full-time thrower, Ted Burdon, had warned me two years previously that he intended to retire at sixty-five, as he wished to end his career still in full command of his skills. For some time I had been trying to recruit an extra thrower, but without success. Throwing had ceased to be a recognised method of production in the industry and it was evident that young men who had learned to throw while at art school, did not wish to work in a factory. Throwing had to give way to casting but, thanks to Ted's forethought, we had ample time in which to produce a large range of models. I had these thrown on the wheel in a double thickness which was needed to withstand the pressure of a plaster cast being taken. I then watched my senior turner, Fred Pickstock, finish each piece on the lathe, scrutinising the balance of the curves to obtain the exact shape that I required. In order to maintain the character of our productions, I continued with the process of hand-turning after casting, which eliminated all traces of the seam left by the junction of the two parts of the mould. Ultimately, many of our shapes were actually

A group of miniature vases with my new ashtrays, 1965.

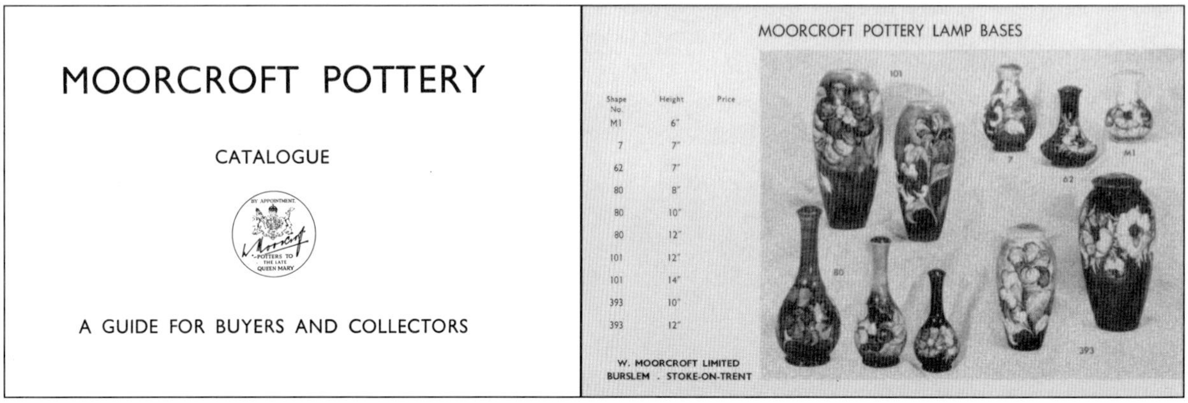

Cover and page from the first Moorcroft black and white catalogue, 1966.

A substantial extension of our lamp base business in the home market came through Charles Bristol of Birmingham, who offered lamps either with a plain silk shade or a parchment shade painted with a reproduction of the floral decoration.

improved as they were not subject to variations caused by the consistency of the clay or the mood of the thrower.

In 1960 we booked a summer holiday at the Fistral Bay Hotel in Newquay and had great expectations for surfing, but Liz became pregnant which limited her performance on the surfboard. My most vivid memory of the holiday is the drive from Staffordshire to Cornwall. It was a long way, as in 1960 there were no motorways or bypasses through towns except for Taunton, which was notoriously congested. To get a good start, we went to my sister's flat in Worcester the evening before and after a few hours sleep, started our journey at 3am. As dawn broke we were driving through the Cotswolds. The countryside was a spectacle of golden beauty thrown into relief by long shadows from the rising sun. Passing through small towns, tall historic buildings in the main squares seemed like the backdrop to stage sets in the theatre as, in the absence of parked vehicles, they were visible from the ground upwards. The year went on. Liz blossomed and, after a somewhat disrupted Christmas in Mansfield where arrangements had been made for the forthcoming event, Sara was born on the 29th December – a truly beautiful baby. I was speechless, not through shock but because of an acute bout of laryngitis and so had to keep my distance.

In the spring of 1961 I bought my second Ford Zephyr Convertible, complete with power-operated hood. It was pale lime green with cream upholstery and cost, including the radio (an extra in those days), £1150. I had bought my first all-white one in 1955 – a similar model had been featured in a Diana Dors' film. It was a magnificent car for the summer holidays because, with the roof down, the paraphernalia from the beach could be thrown in willy-nilly with the passengers of all ages clambering on top. Elisabeth's father Tiny, (a man of small stature but massive intellect), worked at the headquarters of British Rail in London and lived in a flat in Swiss Cottage. This was an ideal *pied à terre* as we could drive down the M1, along Finchley Road, and park the car outside the flat. Our favourite London trip included the Winter Exhibition at Burlington House where we saw the works of Goya, Millais, and Russell Flint in successive years. Each of these painters had previously been stereotyped in my mind by a few, well-known paintings. Seeing many of their works, my eyes were opened, especially by the delicacy and finesse of some of Goya's portraits.

We took three summer holidays in Borth, just north of Aberystwyth, where I had been as a child some thirty years before. It had not changed much. With four miles of sandy beach, it was ideal for children and the high tide mark was a stone's throw across the road from the hotel. We met families with girls of the same age as Jean and Sheila and, wet or fine, had daily bathing parties. Occasionally Elisabeth's parents joined us and travelled from London on the Cambrian Express by a circuitous route from Paddington. The engine had a semi-circular title board displayed proudly on the front of its boiler, and emitted clouds of steam as it chugged along the single line into Borth Station.

Sheila, Liz, myself and Jean with baby Sara, in the garden of my sister, Beatrice's flat in Worcester, 1961.

As the decade progressed, our circle of friends grew and our social life was widened by drinks and dinner parties, and formal dances including the Golf Club dance, the Hockey Club dance and the Keele University Ball. The latter went on until dawn and I remember on one occasion, when Princess Margaret was there, we were almost deafened by a group called Cream; but as the night went on the tempo slowed and couples could be seen dancing languidly, leaning on each other for support. I enjoyed these functions but having grown up with the foxtrot, the quickstep and the waltz, I found the barbaric gyrations of the twist rather intimidating. At home, Liz thought nothing of entertaining over thirty guests and served curry in a giant punch bowl made by Moorcroft for the coronation of King George VI. After nearly thirty years the custom of having lunch at the Grand Hotel in Hanley came to an end because the price of lunch was increased to the exorbitant sum of 11s 6d. We transferred to the restaurant in Lewis's Department Store where we had a reserved table by the door leading on to the roof garden, and ate a three course lunch for 5s.

In 1965 Liz was pregnant again, and Beatrice took Jean and Sheila to Britanny so that Liz and I could have a quiet holiday with only Sara to look after. We received a postcard from Jean saying, 'We are having a wonderful time. Auntie Bea has lost all sorts of things, including the way.' On 12th October, after delays which stretched my mother-in-law's nerves to the limit, Lise arrived. I was just finishing my lunch at Lewis's when I received a message from home that things were about to happen. I set off immediately and on arrival at the entrance to the maternity ward, the first thing we saw was a large container with the inscription 'Put Your Litter Here'! My laughter was not appreciated.

With the increase in our family we had to rethink our ideas for summer holidays and our thoughts went back to Trearddur Bay where, in 1965, we had spent a week with Ted and Dorothy Manson, known as Uncle Ted and Auntie Dorothy as they were lifelong friends of my wife's parents. With the help of the infallible Auntie Dorothy we succeeded in renting Berwyn for the month of August 1967, and this became our annual holiday home for the next twelve years. Berwyn was a basic stone-built house with plenty of room and no frills. It stood in an acre of ground and had been built by Mr Thomas who owned the Trearddur Bay Stores. His widow, a redoubtable character, lived in a flat built on to the house. Berwyn stood high above the road and we used to boast that you could see the sea from every room, including the lavatory. In front of the house was a large flat lawn, which must have been levelled at some time for a tennis court. My immediate thoughts went to croquet, a game that I had never before had the chance to play. We duly bought a croquet set from Hamley's and as time passed, a yearly ritual demanded that the hoops were set out immediately on our arrival. Games of croquet gave hours of pleasures to us all, marred only by accusations of cheating, as I never succeeded in getting a book of rules. Berwyn was always full. In addition to the family, we had *au pairs* from Switzerland; friends came to stay; the girls' friends came to stay; my in-laws came to stay, as did my sister, Beatrice. The house became more like a hotel every year and Liz was an absolute genius in the way she ran it. I just ran the bar!

Lise and myself in our boat at Porth y Castell.

During August, life in Trearddur was dominated by the Trearddur Bay Sailing Club. This was a closely knit society who had been coming to their holiday houses in August since the early 1900s when the club was formed. One generation followed the other by teaching their offspring to sail almost as soon as they could walk. The daily races were run in accordance with strict protocol and it seemed most appropriate that these events coincided with the season at Cowes. The great difference lay in the size of the Trearddur Bay sailing craft which did not exceed sixteen foot but the Half Raters, G.P's Myths and Kadetts (for the very young), were a picturesque sight as they circled the bay awaiting the starting gun from the flagstaff on the headland. We had a boat but it had no sails – it was a pram dinghy which I bought second-hand from the local chandlery. Virtually unsinkable, it was perfect for rowing hour after hour in the bay of Porth y Castell.

Most days were spent on the beach with a variety of picnic lunches bought each day from the Trearddur Bay Stores. Life was one long extended-family party, on and off the beach. There were the Mansons, parents of Janet and Peter – he liked to claim that Liz was the first woman he slept with because they briefly shared a cot when they were six months old! Then the Nelsons, known as the 'Admiralty' with offspring Judy, Andrew and Janet. Alan Shelley, the director of Shelley China, and Tony Parkes were brothers-in-law as their wives, Judith and Susan, were sisters – with their seven children. Peter Taylor of Louis Taylor's, the auctioneers, and his wife Doreen, had a house in Trearddur with their daughters, Diana and Patsy, and their son, Philip, who was my daughter Sheila's boyfriend.

Patsy married Ted Turner and eventually added three more to the party, Emma, Julia and Sara. Dorothy Thompson, whose husband died suddenly in the late 1960s, had a luxurious bungalow on Ravenspoint just above Porth y Castell and expected us to come for drinks on Sunday morning – her son, Alistair, spent all his time sailing. Peter Taylor, Tony and Ted Turner were my golfing partners.

They weren't all there all the time, but there were always enough of us to provide a gaggle of children on the beach indulging in the seaside pursuits of fishing in rock pools, digging in the sand, paddling, bathing or just getting wet by falling into the sea while the adults, in a vegetative state, sat chatting. So long as I could swim every day and escape for the occasional round of golf, I was happy. In the course of the month there were outbursts of rain, tempest and even human tantrums, but it is the memory of long, hot days which endure.

A catalogue with colour cover illustrating *Coral Hibiscus*, produced in 1972 and used throughout the seventies.

Overseas Travel

The idea of Coral Hibiscus on the ivory background came quite by chance…

The euphoria of gaining control of Moorcroft in 1960 gave way to anti-climax in the second half of the decade. Although my new designs had attracted interest at trade fairs, they did not provide the extra turnover needed to fill the gap left by the end of tableware production. It was, therefore, a welcome opportunity when a trade mission to North America was promoted by the Board of Trade and the Pottery Manufacturers Federation for January 1968. I was one of a party of twelve, headed by Sam Jerrett, director of the Federation, and we set off on the 5th January. Because of bad weather, our departure from Manchester Airport was delayed by six hours. Unknown to me, Lise, aged two-and-a-half years, had fallen and broken her leg before I had even taken off. Liz, unhappy about the treatment at the hospital had contacted my friend, Dennis Wainwright, a leading orthopaedic surgeon, who put everything in order and set her mind at rest.

Our trade mission arrived at Kennedy Airport at midnight New York time, after a twenty hour trip, and headed for the Roosevelt Hotel on Madison Avenue. With the added disadvantage of jet lag, New York was disappointing, appearing dirty under a covering of slushy snow and I was not sorry to move on to Atlantic City the following day where the focus of our trip was the Atlantic City Trade Fair, held there each year. The sale of giftware in the United States is handled almost entirely by 'jobbers' (the American term for wholesalers) and the other members of the party were represented at the Fair through this channel. Left to my own devices, I made my way around what seemed to be a vast conglomeration of junk from worldwide markets, interspersed here and there by exclusive merchandise. One particular item I remember was a small plate described as First Limited Edition of 10,000 pieces! It was a great relief to escape for an hour to stroll in the sunshine on the famous shoreline boardwalk. Although there was no prospect of obtaining orders, my time was not wasted as I made contact with Ebeling and Reuss of Philadelphia, a firm of distributors whose business extended from coast to coast, who promised to visit me at the factory when they came to England in the spring.

Leaving the party in Atlantic City, my next destination was Toronto. I was told by an experienced traveller that the best way to get there was via a local flight from Atlantic City to Newark Airport, then a helicopter flight from Newark direct to the John F. Kennedy Airport for the flight to Toronto. The helicopter flight was spectacular. It was a crystal clear day and we flew directly over New York, touching down at the Manhattan Heliport on the way. Canada was a completely different proposition from America as we had been trading with the leading retailers for years. In Toronto we had substantial accounts with Eaton's, The Robert Simpson Co., and Henry Birks. Eaton's was still controlled by the family and I had morning coffee with Bob Eaton. While in Toronto I stayed at the Royal York Hotel, which provided a headquarters

My new drawing of *Coral Hibiscus*, 1968.

from which I was able to make day trips to London, Ontario, and Hamilton. After a week of heavy snow and sub-zero temperatures in Toronto, I set off for St. Louis, spending a day in Chicago en route, in the course of which I visited the vast Marshall Field Store where I bought a diaphanous nightie for Liz and found the inspiration for a range of oval pieces which I put into production during the following year. This proved to be the most important part of my trip as the foundation was laid for the *Coral Hibiscus*, in a discussion with the buyer at Styx, Baer and Fuller, a department store, which sold Moorcroft. During my travels I had made a point of studying the furnishing departments in the big stores where the colour schemes were almost invariably based on shades of brown and orange, often with a background of natural wood. I realised that we had to produce something which was completely free of the blues, pinks and purples which dominated so many Moorcroft decorations. My discussion with the buyer at Styx, Baer and Fuller confirmed this, and we agreed that my *Hibiscus* would be an ideal motif. After a period of trial and error, I produced a coral-coloured flower with a sepia centre on an olive green background – no trace of blue. The colours were right, but the effect of the coral was overwhelmed by the green, so I redrew all the designs, increasing the area of the flowers in relation to the background. The success of this new colour scheme was illustrated by the effect on our business with Henry Birks of Canada. Our sales had dwindled to their five main stores but when Hazen Wright, their group buyer, saw the new *Hibiscus* he immediately put it into twenty-five stores who sent repeat orders within the year. The idea of *Coral Hibiscus* on the ivory background came quite by chance. I had a client in Geneva, a South African woman called Sally Sklaar, who owned a gallery specialising in Georgian silver but bought pieces of Moorcroft to augment her displays. These included lamp bases which, incidentally, she asked me to sign on the front so that my initials would be visible. These I applied discreetly on a leaf within the decoration. She saw my *Coral Hibiscus*, which she liked, but asked me to make some lamp bases for her on an ivory background. I was so pleased with the result that I included one or two in our display at the Harrogate Gift Fair. We were immediately asked whether our regular giftware was available in the same decoration, and it never looked back.

In the spring of 1968, Ebeling and Reuss came to the factory as promised and we duly appointed them as our sole distributors for the United States. When I took George Ebeling out to lunch, he was delighted to find apple pie and cream on the menu as, having no natural cream in America, this was a treat he always looked forward to when visiting England. Their order for samples alone was, by our standards, a large one. Ebeling and Reuss had thirteen showrooms and their substantial stock orders took up all the slack in our production, giving us the psychological advantage of making other clients wait for deliveries. As an aid to sales George Ebeling persuaded me to produce a small leaflet, the first time we had done so, describing the essential features of Moorcroft and the methods of production. On its cover was the slogan 'Made by hand in England for collectors around the world' which has remained in use to the present day.

In 1970 my production of *flambé* came to an end owing to the introduction of natural gas. Its properties were very different from those of coal gas and failed to produce the

Briefing paintresses over colouring. Facing are Mary Etheridge, Glenys Mullock and Gwyneth Hibbitt. Mary and Gwyneth are still working at the Moorcroft factory.

colours that we required from reduction firing in the kiln. The local gas board were very helpful and sent their representatives to see me. When I gave them a demonstration of our firing they were horrified and alarmed by our primitive methods. They gave me access to their local research department but to no avail. This sad end may have been a blessing in disguise as we had been coming under increased pressure to discontinue the coal firing of the muffle kiln in order to comply with the Clean Air Act and I doubt very much whether the process would have been tolerated by the Safety at Work inspectorate had it ever been observed. The end of *flambé* production may have been sad but it was probably beneficial to the profitability of the company rather than the reverse. The process would never have stood up to accurate costing. The kiln was fired at intervals of three weeks and most pieces went through twice if not three times. It provided a challenge to achieve the almost impossible with sheer virtuosity as the measure of success.

Another trade mission was planned for 1971 starting at Atlantic City then on to British Columbia and California. This time I was fully occupied in Atlantic City as Ebeling and Reuss were exhibiting and I had to meet all their salesmen. They were mostly enthusiastic except for one Italian American wearing a pale blue suit, who told me he had dreaded meeting me as he did not sell any Moorcroft because he did not like it. I assured him that if that was the case he never would, and we parted good friends.

Before going to the west coast I arranged a three-day trip to Bermuda where we had built up a substantial business with Masters who had one of the exclusive stores on Front Street in Hamilton, where the cruise liners docked. While there, I managed to spend a day on the Bermuda Ferry, island hopping. I sketched hibiscus flowers which grew in the wild everywhere. To my delighted surprise I found a coral-coloured hibiscus complete with a sepia centre, just as the colour scheme which I had thought was a figment of my imagination. Bermuda was alive with exotic flowers and I asked whether any particular flower was associated with the island. I was told that their national flower was the white Easter Lily which I used for my *Bermuda Lily* design. This became one of my favourites because the white flower on the olive green was totally different from our general productions. A Japanese buyer visiting the factory stroked a vase gently and commented, 'Lovely gift for young lady.' I used only one other flower from Bermuda and this on a very small scale – the pale yellow allamander, which I applied to a small oblong box, but I was unable to visualise it as a full-scale motif.

I left the balmy shores of Bermuda and took a long flight to Vancouver arriving in the early hours of Sunday morning. After a good sleep and a quiet day, I went for a walk. The temperature was dropping fast with the odd flake of snow in the air. By morning, it was fifteen inches deep and Vancouver was paralysed. I made three phone

Albert Nixon, biscuit placer and loyal craftsman for over thirty years.

calls for appointments and was told on each occasion, 'Sorry, there's no-one in yet.' I then called Mr McGregor of the Hudson Bay Co., who said, 'I'm a prairie man. These buggers have no idea what snow is.' Normal life gradually returned. We had always done good business in Vancouver and I was entertained extremely well. When dining with two directors of Woodward's Stores, I was invited to spend a day on Danny Glanville's boat. I discreetly asked who Danny Glanville was. 'First there is God, then Charles Woodward who owns the joint and will be down on his ranch, and then there's Danny Glanville.' The boat was a sixty-four foot luxury motor cruiser custom-built to his own design from stem to stern, and kept moored at the Royal Vancouver Yacht Club just ten minutes away from his office. We spent the day cruising up the coastline of British Columbia. Relaxing in a stateroom thirty-four feet long and furnished like a hotel lounge with a huge windscreen at one end, Danny sat at his controls with room for his charts on one side and a large gin and tonic on the other. He said he had it designed this way because he had tired of navigating from a bridge on top, while everyone enjoyed themselves inside. Down below was a lavishly equipped kitchen galley where thick lobster soup was served as the main course for our lunch.

From Vancouver I flew down to San Francisco where the idea of the factory shop was born. I walked through Chinatown to Fisherman's Wharf and found the Cannery, an old, rough-brick factory converted for the sale of exclusive gifts in patio surroundings. It reminded me of our biscuit warehouse which had hardly been used since we finished coal firing in 1960. My next flight was to Los Angeles and as we approached the city, a fellow passenger

My brother John talking to visitors at the firemouth of the bottle-oven on the occasion of the opening of the factory shop, 25th November 1971.

The Blackpool Fair 1972, showing the Centennial Collection with the first display of *Pansy Nouveau* to the left. The pottery section now transferred from the Imperial Hotel to the Golden Mile Centre.

COLOURS IN WHICH THE SIX PIECES
OF THE W. MOORCROFT CENTENNIAL COLLECTION
ARE AVAILABLE

B–Dark Blue G–Green Y–Yellow
W–Woodsmoke Blue CH–Coral Hibiscus

Item	Size	Decoration		Colours			
Vase	80	10″	Orchid	B	Y	W	6.25
Plate	783	10″	Clematis	B	G	W	3.10
Vase	869	9½″	Hibiscus	B	Y	CH	9.00
Bowl	246	9¾″	Hibiscus	B	G	CH	4.50
Vase	32	5″	Anemone	B	G	Y	2.50
Comport	205	5″	Hibiscus	B	G	CH	2.05

W. MOORCROFT LIMITED
Sandbach Road BURSLEM Stoke-on-Trent ST6 2DQ

THE
W. MOORCROFT
CENTENNIAL COLLECTION

THE W. MOORCROFT CENTENNIAL COLLECTION is a group of pieces which have been specially backstamped to commemorate the centenary of the birth of WILLIAM MOORCROFT, artist and potter, the originator of MOORCROFT POTTERY

COMMEMORATIVE BACKSTAMP

Six pieces only in the shapes and decorations as illustrated will bear the commemorative backstamp. These will be limited to one thousand of each shape but there will be a choice of three colours as listed overleaf.

A four page leaflet for the Centennial Collection, 1972.

drew my attention to the famous smog which hung like a huge yellow blanket, obscuring everything beneath it. I had been advised to contact the British Consul on arrival and was invited to a cocktail party at his residence on my first evening. The party was large, made up mainly of businessmen with a rather one-track line of conversation which usually came round to the leading question, 'How big is your plant!' My evasive reply was invariably, 'Not as big as you think.'

I spent a great deal of my time in the showroom of Ebeling and Reuss. When I told them that we used to make things especially for Shreve of San Francisco they said, 'We have a great respect for your royal family but out here "Made for Shreve of San Francisco" means more than "Made for the Queen of England."' After three days hard work with a quick glimpse of Hollywood and Beverly Hills, my trip was finished and I boarded the Pan Am *Clipper* (an early 747) for my journey home. My travelling companion worked for Poole Pottery where he was in charge of the factory seconds' shop and he told me that he had been in trouble with his boss because of his claim that they made more money in the shop than was made in the factory. During the long flight we discussed the merits and problems of a factory shop and I could see an opportunity which was too good to miss. Plans rapidly fell into place.

We landscaped our overgrown field to provide a car park and had the factory painted a Californian sand colour. The warehouse was cleared round the biscuit oven and we found a steeplejack to point the chimney inside and out. Then we were ready for business (see page 66).

By now there were very few bottle ovens left and from the beginning, we advertised the features of the bottle-oven and shop, which met with immediate success. My brother, John, was a tower of strength in implementing these plans as he supervised all the operational details while I got on with running the factory and when the shop opened his wife, Gill, took on its management.

When George Ebeling came to the factory in the spring of 1971, he saw one of my father's early *Pansy* vases with light green colouring on a white background which he said he would like me to use as the basis of a new range. I explained that I was not prepared to reproduce my father's early designs, but I would redraw the pansies in a similar style and capture the colour factor with a very pale green background. George was pleased with the result and gave it the rather pretentious name of *Pansy Nouveau* which I concluded, was a cross between 'New Pansy' and 'Art Nouveau', well-suited to the American market. It was reasonably successful but the colour used for the pale green background was very sensitive to marks and when, at the end of 1972, George suggested that we should discontinue it, I was pleased to agree.

As Christmas 1972 approached I was not well but kept going, not wishing to interrupt the festive season. Eventually I collapsed with a serious bowel infection and after five days on the danger list, stayed on a drip feed for quite a while longer. This was followed by a thrombosis in my leg brought on by dehydration, and I had to rest every afternoon for the next three months. With hindsight, this unpleasant experience was a blessing in disguise. With good living in the 1960s, I had gained a lot of weight which was wiped out overnight and I made up my mind that it would never return, and the three months enforced rest gave my whole system a new lease of life.

During the 1970s, the girls were growing up. In 1972 Jean qualified as a nurse at St. Bartholomew's Hospital in London and in the same year, married Stephen Potter. They had met in London but Steve had lived near to Trentham as a child and had actually come to Easedale as a young boy scout for 'Bob-a-job week'. We staged a 'quiet' wedding using the garage (which was later to become May's flat) for the reception with an awning leading down the drive. Roland, an ex-steward from the SS Queen Mary and Trentham Golf Club, did the catering aided by his wife. He administered the bar with such enthusiasm that a bottle of champagne was consumed for each of the forty-eight guests. Sheila went to East Anglia University in 1970 to read German and European Studies and after spending her third year in Berlin, graduated in 1974.

Changes were also taking place in Moorcroft. Two exhibitions in the 1970s completely changed the concept of early Moorcroft pottery. In 1963 it had been seen as 'second-hand pots'. By 1973 it was reaching equal status with antiques. The first exhibition was at the Victoria and Albert Museum in 1972 when, to mark the centenary of his birth, they allotted a whole gallery to the work of William Moorcroft and during the next twelve months, a part of this exhibition went on tour to a number of provincial museums.

A view of the works showing the winding gear of the old Sneyd Colliery from where we bought coal for the kilns, 1972.

MOORCROFT
For the convenience of Christmas Shoppers our
BOTTLE OVEN & SECONDS SHOP
will be open on
SATURDAY MORNINGS, 9th, 16th DECEMBER
from 9.30 - 12.30
in addition to our Normal Opening Hours
Mon.-Fri. 10 a.m. - 12.30 p.m. and 1.30 - 3.30 p.m.

A WIDE VARIETY OF GIFT ITEMS
from 33p to £2.75

Moorcroft Pottery, Sandbach Road, Cobridge

An advertisement for the new factory shop, *The Evening Sentinel*, 1972.

POST CARD.
WENGERS·LTD.
Manufacturers·of·Colours·&·Chemicals
for Potters Glassmakers & Enamellers on Metal
ETRURIA,
STOKE-ON-TRENT,
ENGLAND.

Jean and myself at her wedding, with Sara and Lise, Longton, 26th October 1972.

Ceramic art, renowned for its rich brilliance by
MOORCROFT
A group of small gift items. Vases 3" to 6", Candy Box and 3" Coaster in "Hibiscus" and "Clematis" decorations
Every piece an investment

J. W. Mears
34-40 Derby Road, Long Eaton
Telephone: 4936

If it's:-

ANTLER	LUGGAGE
CARLTON	TABLE-WARE
KIENZLE	CLOCKS
McLAREN	HAND-BAGS
MOORCROFT	POTTERY
OLD HALL	STAINLESS STEEL
PARAGON	CHINA
PARKER	PENS
PLATIGNUM	PENS
PAPER-MATE	PENS
ROAMER	WATCHES
RONSON	LIGHTERS
REMINGTON	RAZORS & CLOCKS
SALISBURY	CHINA
SEIKO	WATCHES
SMITHS	CLOCKS & WATCHES
VINERS	STAINLESS STEEL
WEBB CORBETT	CUTGLASS
WEYMOUTH AMERICAN	HAND-BAGS
ABBEYDALE	CHINA
SHEAFFER	PENS

It's Mears

Let us quote you for your next presentation

An advertisement for Moorcroft stockist F.W. Mears, a great *flambé* enthusiast who bought some of my best pieces which he sold in a small shop in a Long Eaton mining village, after accepting payment in instalments, *Derbyshire Life*, 1972.

The second exhibition was staged by Richard Dennis in the galleries of the Fine Art Society, New Bond Street in London, and was entitled 'William Moorcroft and Walter Moorcroft 1897-1973'. The most important feature of this exhibition was the catalogue which Richard Dennis and Paul Atterbury produced for the occasion. This was the first comprehensive record of Moorcroft pottery and its origins to be published and provided information which was essential for would-be collectors. The far-reaching effect of these exhibitions was reflected in an invitation which I received from Macy's of New York to reproduce some of the early Moorcroft designs for sale in their store in Times Square. I declined on the grounds that such work would not be original, and it could well be regarded as an inferior reproduction.

The Blackpool Fair 1975, the Golden Mile Centre. The display includes the new *Eastern Lily* and *Bermuda Lily*.

The Blackpool Fair Moves to Birmingham

With entirely new, shocking-pink flowers...it was Moorcroft with a difference...

During the early seventies the city of Birmingham had embarked on an ambitious scheme to create a National Exhibition Centre on a very large scale. Trade Promotion Services, still headed by Elkan Simons, immediately recognised the potential and took steps to transfer the whole of the Blackpool Fair to the new location. I had great admiration for the ability of Elkan Simons as an organiser and as soon as we were officially advised of the Fair, I requested application forms for space. In due course they arrived and I sent my application together with a cash deposit by return. Three months later Elkan Simons came to Stoke-on-Trent to persuade hesitant manufacturers that it was safe to abandon Blackpool in favour of Birmingham. In the meanwhile, as the result of my foresight, we had acquired the first space immediately inside the main entrance, and have kept it ever since.

After I had made the initial contact, John built up a firm liaison with Percy Sweetser, Elkan Simon's right-hand man, to iron out any administration problems. He also relieved me of the logistics of setting up the stand and updating it from year to year, which he did with great skill, supported by his wife Gill. For the period of the Fair we stayed at Penns Hall Hotel in Sutton Coldfield and were a good family team.

Preliminary sketches of *Magnolia* and composition of design on a $9^1/_2$ins vase, 1975.

The first International Gifts Fair at the N.E.C. opened in February 1976 and was the ideal setting in which to launch my *Magnolia* design. The idea of using a magnolia as a new motif came in April 1975, from the cover of a gardening magazine. I knew that some of the best magnolias outside Kew Gardens grew at Hodnet Hall in Shropshire, the home of the Heber Percy's, which opened its grounds to the public. I phoned to ask when I could see them at their best and was told that they should peak in the first week of May. So, off I went armed with sketchbook and camera. Though individually beautiful, the flowers suggested regimental rows of light bulbs sprouting from the almost bare branches but when I inadvertently hung my camera on a branch, I saw an inside view of the flower which I made into a central feature of the decoration. With entirely new, shocking-pink flowers on a dark blue background, it was Moorcroft with a difference and within eighteen months it had been sold in all five continents as well as enjoying a major promotion by Mutsukoshi of Tokyo.

In 1975 Liz went back to work. She received a letter from the North Staffordshire Health Authority inviting qualified occupational therapists to offer their services on a part-time basis to overcome the shortage of staff. She worked two mornings a week at the North Stafford Royal Infirmary in Stoke-on-Trent, commenting that she really enjoyed it and, what's more, she got paid! The significance of this situation came ten years later when, without once seeking promotion, she was appointed District Occupational Therapist with some twenty-two hospitals under her administration.

MOORCROFT

SCHOOL LEAVERS

ARE INVITED TO APPLY FOR A SITUATION TO TRAIN FOR

FREEHAND PAINTING

Interesting handwork in pleasant surroundings

Apply —

MOORCROFT POTTERY

SANDBACH ROAD, COBRIDGE

Telephone 24323

With a good order book we advertised for paintresses to meet the demand. *The Evening Sentinel*, February 1976.

The first Birmingham Fair with my new *Magnolia* design in the foreground, February 1976.

Advertising for a small group of jewellery for which I engraved the motif in the mould and produced with reasonable success for two or three years, Harrogate Gift Fair, 1976.

In 1976 I was invited to become President of Trentham Golf Club, a non-executive appointment in recognition of long support of the club and its activities. (I had joined as a junior member in 1928.) In the course of my term of office George Dring, the secretary, gave me staunch support. My appointment happened to coincide with the year when he was the senior Club Secretary in the Midlands. Each year, the Midland Club Secretaries held a golf tournament and George asked me to provide them with something to play for bearing their insignia, a quill pen crossed with a golf club and a golf ball surrounded by the initials A.S.G.S. (Association of Staffordshire Golf Club Secretaries). I chose a substantial jardiniere as a vehicle for the design and, realising that the golfing world would not want flowery detail, I placed their insignia on the front and a *Bermuda Lily* on the back, all on an olive green background. It shook George rigid! The A.S.G.S. was equally impressed and the trophy has become a treasured possession.

MOORCROFT

BOTTLE OVEN AND SECONDS SHOP

A wide variety of Pottery Gifts
VASES • BOWLS • ASHTRAYS • BOXES
JARDINIERES
LAMP BASES A good selection of shapes and designs including new colours.
EARLY MOORCROFT — Collectors Items 1914 — 1959.
Opening hours: Mon. - Fri. 10 a.m. — 12.30 p.m. — 1.30 — 3.30 p.m.

CAR PARK and ADMISSION FREE

SANDBACH ROAD, COBRIDGE, STOKE-ON-TRENT

Advertisement for the first Moorcroft sale including my father's 'trials', *The Staffordshire Magazine*, 1977.

The Moorcroft Trophy which I made for the Association of Golf Club Secretaries, 1976. When presenting it to them, I remarked that if anyone thought that the shaft of the golf club was slightly bent they should remember that in the days of quill pens they had hickory shafts.

Advertisement in *Tableware International* for the Birmingham Spring Fair, February 1978. The smoker's set was highly acceptable in 1978, with the first of the Moorcroft blue boxes.

On Christmas Eve 1976, after battling with the illness for two years, my father-in-law, Tiny, died of cancer. The following year my mother-in-law, May, had a minor stroke which left no visible effects but meant that she could no longer live on her own. We had a problem.

After various considerations, I arrived at the unique solution of being able to put my mother-in-law into my garage! I had a large garage with a communicating door leading into our kitchen. An architect friend of mine came up with a perfect answer to our problem. A five-feet extension onto the garage provided space for a large bed-sitting room with its own front door and a Georgian bow window facing west. A smaller extension at the rear, provided a kitchen, bathroom and lavatory. The flat was a great success and gave May seven happy years before her death in November 1985.

In 1978, three months before her eighteenth birthday, Sara entered Durham University to read Geography and graduated in 1981. Lise, still a teenager, was studying at St. Dominic's High School and showing considerable talent in the culinary side of Domestic Science. As Lise was the youngest by five years, she was sometimes left out on a limb and often turned to me for sporting activities, and we played all kinds of improvised games. The last was in Tintagel in 1980, when we played badminton over a washing line in our cottage garden and I hung tea towels on the line to stop her from cheating by hitting the shuttlecock underneath.

In 1979 the increased recognition of Moorcroft was demonstrated by a very fine exhibition of early pieces staged by the Ato Gallery in the Seibu Department Store in Tokyo. They had been building up their collection for some time through purchases in the London salerooms and sought my assistance in confirming their authenticity by producing a separate photograph of each item with a declaration on the back for my signature.

The Brink of Disaster

We were overdrawn at the bank and high interest rates aggravated the situation...

As we moved into the 1980s, export markets were beginning to suffer from a strong pound but this did not seem to affect us and in 1981 I was invited by Henry Birks of Canada to go to British Columbia to support a special promotion in their Vancouver and Victoria stores. I spent three days in Vancouver and three in Victoria where I visited Geoff Reynolds whose father had emigrated from England to start his business there in 1934 and had traded with us ever since. While in Geoff's shop I bought some *papier-mâché* miniature boxes made in Kashmir, to take home as gifts. They seemed an ideal new item for Moorcroft and, on my return, I had six shapes modelled with matching miniature trays and designed them with *Anemone, Hibiscus, Magnolia* and *Lily* motifs, which proved a great success.

The trip to British Columbia was a wonderful experience. I met many interesting people and had a great rapport with the staff of the Birks stores, but Birks had overbought from us and from other participants in the promotion and in 1982, with a recession setting in, the value of orders plummeted. The recession spread rapidly and affected the whole pottery industry. Within two years about a third of the total workforce had been laid off.

After gaining her degree at Durham, Sara had come to work at the factory in 1981 to obtain general experience in the running of the business but, with the recession setting in, the prospects were disappointing and she asked if I would mind if she went back to university for a twelve-month teaching course. She went to Nottingham University where she was lucky to get a small grant before Keith Joseph, the Education Secretary, clamped down on them. She came top of her year and met Paul who was studying the same course after obtaining his degree in History at Cambridge University.

Lise was now eighteen and her school days were over. She decided that she would rather study art than continue with domestic science, and embarked upon a foundation year at the local technical college. It was evident that she had made the right choice because her artistic ability blossomed and, at the end of the year, she gained entry to the Central School of Art in London to study ceramics. She met Shaun who was studying animation at St. Martin's and after a year in a hall of residence, they shared a maisonette in Southfields.

By 1983, Moorcroft Pottery was in trouble. We were overdrawn at the bank and high interest rates aggravated the situation. Various options were considered but did not develop and at the beginning of 1984 we were on the brink of disaster. We made contact with the Churchill Group, owned by the Roper family. I had known Peter Roper for many years and the factories were run by his three sons, Michael the potter, Stephen the salesman and Andrew the accountant. They had the largest privately-owned business in the industry making cheap earthenware and had decided to diversify.

Discussions followed but when the final agreement was on the table, I received a shock. I was to part with two-thirds of my shares at a peppercorn price and my salary was to be reduced from £14,000 to £8,000, the balance to be made up out of profits. As there were no profits, my position would have been untenable. When I rejected the offer, I felt like a poker player using his last chips. The three brothers withdrew from the room and in due course returned with a fresh offer. I could keep my salary but I must sell the rest of my shares and resign my position as Managing Director. I was cleaned out. However, at least we were still in business and I was very grateful for their support. John took my place and, during the time with Churchill, we worked well together. Later, when the company was re-formed, he became a very good ambassador, travelling the world on its behalf.

In contrast to the traumatic changes in my working life, events at home provided happy relief. Sara had done well at Nottingham, Lise was settling down at the Central School of Art in London and Liz and I celebrated our Silver Wedding. With great generosity Jean, Sheila, Sara and Lise each subscribed £25 in travel vouchers so that Liz and I could have a romantic weekend in Paris, but Liz had always wanted to to go Crete. She added the extra from her hard-earned savings and we booked a week at the Hermes Hotel in Aghios Nikolaus. Liz overcame her fear of flying with the help of a window seat in the smoking area of the aircraft and a timely supply of gin and tonic. The holiday was a great success and she achieved her ambition of visiting Knossos. The weather was perfect and while sunbathing by the hotel swimming pool, I sketched geraniums – they appealed to me because their petals had a different formation from those normally seen in Britain.

A *Geranium* sketch, Crete, 1984.

In the autumn of 1984, Sara and Paul each took up their first teaching appointments near Huddersfield and Bradford respectively. On 27th July the following year, they were married at Trentham Parish Church and we celebrated the wedding with a marquee in our back garden on one of the few fine days during a wet summer. They settled in Brighouse in Yorkshire.

After our trip to Crete, I had produced a *Geranium* design which gave me great pleasure and I followed this with a *Campanula* design. Unfortunately, what promised to be two effective designs were somewhat spoiled by trying to produce them too cheaply. I also did two butterfly designs on lamp bases. This happened because I saw a sketch of a butterfly on a vase and my comment was that if we were to have butterflies with a Moorcroft backstamp they must not look as though they were impaled on a board by a pin.

Pencil drawings for my 'Monday, Tuesday, Wednesday' *Tulip* design.

My final design for Churchill was an interesting exercise in producing a lamp base for Marks and Spencer to sell in a pilot scheme in their Marble Arch store. It had to be a completely new motif and we decided on tulips. During a Monday lunchtime I bought some tulips from a Hanley florist and, when completed, I called it my 'Monday, Tuesday, Wednesday' design. The flowers were on my desk and on Monday afternoon I sketched a tight bud, Tuesday a flower half-open and on Wednesday, a fully-open flower. The lamp was finished with salmon-pink flowers on a white background. Sales were disappointing but Marks and Spencer kindly said that it was not our fault, as the entire scheme had failed to come up to their expectations.

Visiting the International Gifts Fair the following year, I saw some virginal white tulips in a vase on the Royal Copenhagen stand and I reproduced my *Tulip* design with a white flower on olive green. It was a very limited edition on a ten inch vase, a seven inch vase, and a ten inch plate.

The Pendulum Swings Back and Retirement

I was proud to be able to claim that from 1898-1986 every piece of Moorcroft had been designed by my father or myself...

Dave Simmons, the Moorcroft distributor in Canada, and myself at the book launch of *Moorcroft – A Guide to Moorcroft Pottery 1897-1993*.

My sister Beatrice, who contributed to the writing of the text of the *Moorcroft* book.

The Moorcroft family attending the launch of *Moorcroft* at Liberty's in 1987. From left, Jean, Sheila, Sara, Lise, Liz and myself.

My brother John and myself at the book launch.

My corner in the old office previously occupied by my father since 1913. The girls from the decorating shop are bringing in their *Moorcroft* books for my signature, 1987.

While we were struggling at the factory, interest from the collector's world was gathering momentum. In September 1985, Richard Dennis, who had organised the 1973 Moorcroft Exhibition in New Bond Street, and Hugh Edwards, an avid collector, decided to produce a comprehensive book on Moorcroft illustrated entirely in colour, with the history of the Pottery written by Paul Atterbury. Our contribution was a marathon photographic session at Easedale. The dining room was the stockroom; each take was assembled in the hall, Richard fired the questions, I supplied details and Hugh took the notes. Prue Cuming took the pictures, the drawing room became the photographic studio and the pantry, the dark room. My mother-in-law was wandering about to see what was going on and the cat was aborting a litter of kittens in the kitchen drawer. All most exciting!

Two years passed. Despite concerted efforts, Churchill decided that we were not a viable proposition and set in motion arrangements for our disposal. Once more we were on the verge of disaster. Various options were considered and discarded, then John phoned Hugh Edwards who replied, 'Give me twenty-four hours and I will form a company.' He contacted Richard Dennis and we were back in business. Richard's wife, Sally, who as Sally Tuffin was a well-known dress designer in the 1960s, was to take over as the Art Director. I was pleased to make her welcome and to have the opportunity to introduce her to some of our ways of working. When handing over the reins to Sally I was proud to be able to claim that from 1898 to 1986, every piece of Moorcroft had been designed by my father or myself.

There was a lot of creative activity in the factory with new designs from Philip Richardson, and members of the staff for whom a competition was staged as a means of selection. This spurred me on to do something on my own account and, mindful of the new wave of collectors, I produced in quick succession, three new designs as limited editions. The first was described as the *Pineapple Plant* owing to a mistaken interpretation of a reference book. At the beginning of October we had spent a week in Menorca where I saw this massive cactus-like plant, which I sketched in some detail. It was a year or so later, when seeing it again on my second visit to Crete, that I discovered the correct name to be *agave giganteum* which is linked with Greek mythology, but that is another story.

Next came *Chestnut Leaves* drawn and photographed during a 'working lunch' in Swynnerton some ten miles from the factory, where I knew from gathering conkers in days gone by, that the trees grew in profusion. Finally, I was asked to design the year plate for 1987. I decided on freesias and paid a special visit to the Bridgemere Garden Centre where I made a few sketches on the spot and took a plant home for detailed reference. To enhance the delicacy of the flowers, I chose yellow for the background.

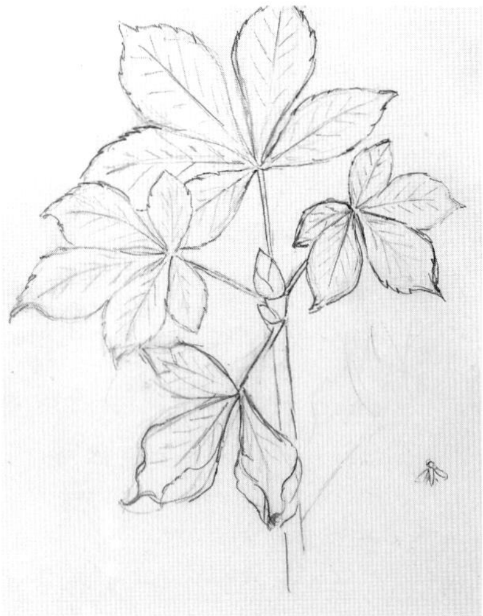

Sketch of *Chestnut Leaves* made at Swynnerton during my working lunch, 1987.

This short burst of artwork was a satisfying prelude to my retirement in March 1987 which was celebrated by a party given by the company in my honour, and where I received a superb presentation plate to mark the occasion. I was invited to 'come on board' on a consultancy basis, including a monthly pay cheque which was more than welcome. It was a great relief to be freed from responsibility and to see the company in such good hands.

At home I was happy to see Liz off each morning to pursue her high-powered job with the Health Service and, two or three times a week, to leave at my leisure to spend a couple of hours at the factory, occupying my time with line-drawings and watercolours of my designs. I observed what was going on with great interest, but only offered advice when asked for it.

In July 1987 Lise received her Honours Degree in Ceramics at the Central School of Art and it came as a great shock to me when I discovered there was no place for her at the factory.

The occasion of my retirement. I am holding a presentation plaque for the benefit of the camera while Patty Booth, who started work at Macintyre's with my father in 1912, stands in the background, 1987.

The front door at Easedale with azalea, clematis and roses.

My new greenhouse in the spring with Morning Glories, dahlias and geraniums.

Our dining room table set with Moorcroft *Powder Blue Tableware* for a family gathering.

I had no regrets about my retirement and soon learned to enjoy it to the full. My garden absorbed an increasing part of my time and I was not really surprised to discover that plants grew far better when fed and watered regularly. To help me on my way, Liz bought me a new greenhouse, which was a great success.

The following year the company asked me if I would make an attempt to produce *flambé* again and a small electric kiln designed for reduction firing was installed in part of the old packing house alongside the factory. My first consideration was that the kiln should not go out through the roof, as injecting gas into a glorified box created, in effect, an unexploded bomb, a very different proposition from a coal-fired muffle kiln with a fifty-foot chimney, which took away all the surplus fumes.

I sought technical advice. The first recommendation was fraught with so many safety valves, inlet valves, outlet valves and automatic cut-outs that it was quite impractical. The next came from a kiln technician whom I had known for many years. He said, rather enigmatically, that he could fulfil my requirements technically but would prefer not to. Then came Brian Madge who was experienced in kiln design at the highest level but still had the mind of a studio potter. His first precaution was to remove the catches from the kiln door to

The 'Studio' side of Brian Madge trials with a 'pot kiln' prior to adapting our box type electric kiln for *flambé* firing.

Flambé: I am applying malodorous paste prior to reduction firing, 1989.

minimise the effect of an explosion, 'It would blow forwards, instead of upwards.' Using propane instead of coal gas, I obtained some moderately successful results, but it became evident that the change of glaze and the nature of the new underglaze colours impaired the purity of colour produced in the past. Eventually, I was asked if I would mind abandoning the project as it was unlikely to be a commercial proposition, and I was only too willing to agree.

In 1989 the Moorcroft Museum was opened at the factory. It appeared as if by magic, carved out of what had been the warehouse for our *Powder Blue Tableware*, by the erection of a dividing wall. With a new roof, a parquet floor and around the walls, the original oak showcases made by Liberty & Co. for Moorcroft exhibitions in the 1920s, the scene was set. This was the realisation of an ambition of Richard Dennis' since he first met me at the factory in the 1960s, and saw a phantasmagoria of old and dirty pots stacked in the pens in our glost warehouse. After the company was re-formed in 1986, Richard spent hours cleaning and sorting pieces which still remained in various parts of the factory, and my brother John had the oak showcases restored and fitted with internal lighting to contain them. With the purchase of a few additional items, a display was completed to show the development of Moorcroft from its beginning to the present day. The museum was officially opened on the 7th June by Arnold Mountford CBE, formerly curator of the City Museum and Art Gallery, with the Lord Mayor and Lady Mayoress of Stoke-on-Trent among the assembled guests.

In 1989, three new large pieces were added to the range of shapes in *Anemone*, and I was asked to design them. I was not satisfied with a rehash of what had been done

The opening of the Moorcroft Museum. From left, Hugh Edwards, John Moorcroft, Richard Dennis, myself, the Mayor and Mayoress of Stoke-on-Trent and the late Arnold Mountford, 1989.

before so I bought a bunch of anemones, which I had much pleasure in charging to the factory. Free from administrative responsibilities, I was able to look at them afresh and realised, amongst other details, that the foliage played a far more important part in their structure than had previously been recognised. When my work on the new shapes was completed, I was told that my new designs made the rest look out-of-date and I was asked to redesign the whole range, which I did in easy stages over the next year. From then on, as extra shapes were added to the *Anemone* or *Magnolia* ranges, I was called upon to supply the artwork and my most recent contribution was three pieces for the 1997 catalogue.

On the 1st December 1990, Lise and Shaun were married in Trentham Church. Lise declared that it was to be a Christmas wedding with *Ding Dong Merrily on High* as one of the hymns and a jazz band to complete the proceedings after the reception. My ancient apple tree in our garden had died so there was room for a larger marquee than we had for Sara's wedding. Apart from the dining area, this accommodated a small dance floor, plus a boisterous jazz band led by Michael Condon, a local jazz enthusiast. Lise produced some very good work in her primitive studio but in 1991 she felt the urge to become involved with the factory and, in March, wrote a letter offering her services. Five months later she received a rejection which, although in accordance with company policy, caused great hurt to her and had a traumatic effect on the family. I found myself with completely split loyalties. I was left precariously balanced with a foot in each camp, divided between my family who were in a state of uncompromising wrath, and the company which had been my life's work for fifty years and continued to provide me with a living. I prefer to avoid voicing judgement on the situation but I found great satisfaction in the ensuing years to see the successful development of Lise's work on one side, and the complete restructuring of the factory on the other.

In 1991, Jean, Steve and family went to live in the United States as Steve had been asked to transfer to the New York Office of the Anglo-American company for

Olive Leake was employed by my father in 1945 at the age of fourteen. She worked for many years as my ware selector and retired in 1996.

Asymmetrical view of *Anemone* flower and bud for my new interpretation of the most traditional Moorcroft flower. It has been in production for over half-a-century.

which he worked. They acquired a lovely house in Southport Connecticut on Long Island Sound from where Steve commuted to New York each day. In May 1993 we visited them; we made trips to New York and they took us for long drives through Connecticut, Massachusetts and Long Island. The weather was wonderful but the twenty-four hour weather programme on television (which we found the most acceptable of the fifty-five channels available) kept referring to 'tornadic activity' in the mid-west, which was the forerunner of the great Mississippi floods which came later in the summer.

We interrupted our stay with Jean and Steve in order to visit our friends Ray and Ann Probst in St. Louis, who have a collection of over 2,000 pieces of Moorcroft. They gave us a wonderful time and as well as heating their swimming pool to over 90° for our benefit, they took us for tours round St. Louis and the surrounding countryside, a hundred miles up the Mississippi and Missouri which were already in flood. Having come so far, we flew on to San Francisco where we spent three fascinating days, before returning to Connecticut for a final week.

In 1995, plans were announced for a Moorcroft Centenary to be celebrated in 1997, a hundred years on from my father's appointment as a designer by James Macintyre of Burslem. I was asked to produce something special to mark the occasion which I willingly agreed to do. It had to be different, and it had to be good. The embryo of an idea had been in my mind for some years but had been set aside as, after my retirement, the production of new Moorcroft designs had become the responsibility first of Sally Tuffin and then, in 1992, Rachel Bishop. Now was my chance to let my idea develop.

Despite our holidays abroad, Anglesey retained a magnetic attraction and regardless of the weather, Liz and I made brief visits several times a year. Returning home in the late afternoon with the weather clearing from the west, the evening sun often illuminated the landscape against the grey backcloth of retreating storm clouds. To frame my impression of the countryside I chose Scots Pines, on account of their height and unusual formation, and I spent several weeks photographing them and drawing them in their natural habitat. Their exposed roots gripped the ground like witches' talons. I was able to work at my leisure in the old packing house where my experimental kiln had been, gradually building up my drawing on the clay. By March 1996, a vase still in the experimental stage had to be ready for the photographer. Asked to name my design, I called it *After the Storm*, which I felt encapsulated the effect and was symbolic of the fluctuations in my life.

Our Christmas tree pot, a seventeen-inch ginger jar which has held a seven foot tree each year for a whole generation. It is cracked and has no lid but serves its purpose well.

The Centenary Year 1997, exceeded all expectations. My *After the Storm* vase was a great success – the limited edition of two hundred was sold out in a week. In February, the first function took place at the Birmingham International Gifts Fair with a cocktail party at the Metropole Hotel in the Exhibition Centre. Liz and I were all but swept off our feet by the enthusiasm of the assembled company.

The launch of a book written by Hugh Edwards under his *nom de plume* Fraser Street, entitled *Moorcroft – The Phoenix Years*, describing the emergence of the company from the ashes, 1986-1997, took place at Liberty's in London on the 20th March 1997. The period of the launch was 12 noon to 7pm. A long queue had formed before the opening time and there was a continual flow of people seeking to buy signed copies of the book. Liz and I had been specially asked to attend and to stay the night in London as the guests of the company. On Hugh's recommendation we stayed at the Athenaeum in an executive room overlooking Hyde Park, which made it a memorable occasion.

In May, Liz and I slipped off to Switzerland to keep a longstanding promise to visit Ursula, who had stayed with us as an *au pair* in the late 1960s and with whom we had kept up a friendship for nearly thirty years. Ursula lived in a small village in the Emmenthal and drove us for miles through the surrounding countryside. While there, we spent a day in Berne with Franziska and Regina who had also stayed with us as *au pairs* but whom we had not met since. To complete our trip we crossed Switzerland to spend a week in Lugano where we had spent our honeymoon in 1959.

We arrived back just in time for the Moorcroft Collectors Club weekend at the factory. This was an outstanding success being fully booked for three days. Once more we met many people who were really pleased to see us. Over lunch we had long conversations with Eric Knowles (an antiques expert on many popular television programmes including *The Antiques Roadshow*), who had been invited to give the introductory lecture at the museum.

The next social occasion was a Centenary Ball arranged to take place on 10th and 11th October with the magician, Paul Daniels and his wife, Debbie McGee, both

Right, *After the Storm* vase, brush drawing on the clay, 1996. Far right, in the decorating shop, keeping an eye on the painting of this special vase.

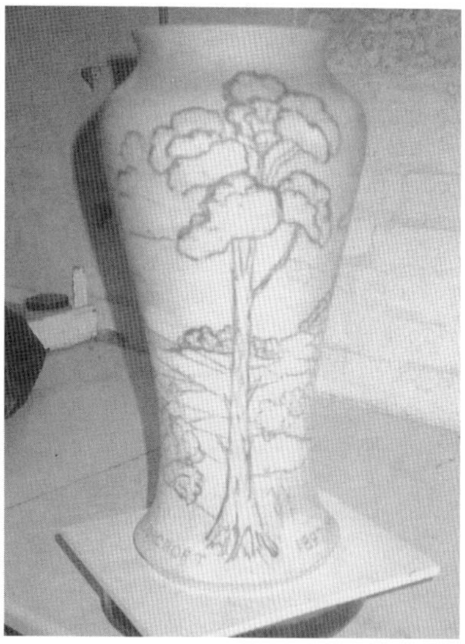

Moorcroft collectors, providing the cabaret. We received invitations to attend on each of the nights. On the first, we sat at a table with Hugh, Maureen and some special guests; on the second night we had a table for ten with a complete family party, including my sister Beatrice.

The Stoke-on-Trent Cultural and Services Department with the full support of W. Moorcroft plc and various collectors, staged a centenary exhibition at the City Museum. This was opened with a private view on the evening of 3rd October. Apart from dignitaries such as the Lord Mayor and Mark Fisher M.P., it was attended by a number of my old employees who greeted me with touching affection. The exhibition was planned to last until mid-January but it was such an outstanding success, breaking all attendance records, that it was extended until the third week in March.

At the beginning of December we had a grand finale to the eventful year. Hugh Edwards asked us if we would like to go to Canada to represent the company at a Centenary Auction to be held by Waddingtons of Toronto, on 6th December. Apart from the experience of first class travel and hotel accommodation, we received wonderful hospitality and met many delightful people. I lost count of the scores of sale catalogues and books presented for my signature, and I was even asked to sign a cigarette packet on which I made a rough sketch to illustrate some special shapes.

Whatever my general activities have been, Moorcroft Pottery has dominated my life and I have said many times, that I did not know whether it was dedication or bloodymindedness that kept me going. I have always been more aware of criticism than adulation and weathered many scathing comments during periods of non-appreciation, especially in the 1930s and the 1950s. One favourable comment which I like to remember was made with a touch of dry humour by Peter Williams, a senior director of Wedgwood, whom I had known for many years. He looked around our exhibit at the Birmingham Fair and, in the terms of a schoolmaster remarked, 'All your own work – very good!'

It is hard to express the depth of feeling aroused by the increased recognition of Moorcroft past and present through the last decade. To this, I must add my gratitude to Liz for her unfailing support and my pride in the success of my daughters, Jean, Sheila and Sara in their various walks of life and Lise, who is gaining recognition as a ceramic artist.

The Moorcroft Centenary provided a perfect conclusion to the first decade of my retirement and the common purpose of successful celebrations provided a catalyst for the settlement of past differences.

Epilogue

With the passage of time my religious faith has faltered in the direction of agnosticism, but one personal prayer still rings true:

Oh! Lord help me to find thy gifts to us in life
The beauty of love
The beauty of living
The beauty of the world.

I have found them all.